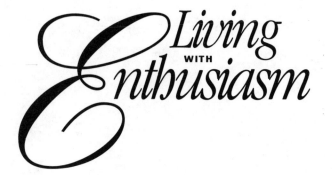

Living
WITH
Enthusiasm

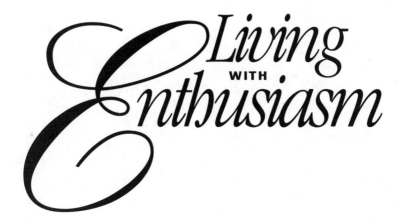

L. TOM PERRY

DESERET BOOK COMPANY
SALT LAKE CITY, UTAH

Library of Congress Cataloging-in-Publication Data

Perry, L. Tom, 1922–
   Living with enthusiasm / by L. Tom Perry.
     p.   cm.
   Includes bibliographical references and index.
   ISBN 1-57345-136-3
   1. Christian life—Mormon authors. 2. Perry, L. Tom, 1922–
I. Title.
BX8656.P39   1996
248.4'89332—dc20   96-580
                                                              CIP

Printed in the United States of America

10 9   8   7   6   5   4   3   2   1

Contents

....

PREFACE

Rₐₗₚₕ Wₐₗdₒ Eₘₑᵣₛₒₙ wᵣₒₜₑ: "Every great and commanding moment in the annals of the world is the triumph of some enthusiasm.... Nothing great was ever achieved without enthusiasm."[1]

Have you ever noticed how much more pleasant it is to be around a person who possesses an enthusiastic spirit? Have you been aware of how much more you respond to an enthusiastic leader or an enthusiastic teacher? It is difficult to be depressed, unhappy, worried, or concerned about the challenges of life if one develops an attitude of attacking each opportunity with an enthusiastic spirit. I believe enthusiasm is a universal talent everyone can acquire.

As I consider my favorite characters in the scriptures—Joseph, Moses, Daniel, Paul, Nephi, and Alma—Joseph always emerges at the top of my list. He overcame rejection, enslavement, and temptation—each of these a difficult challenge—to become the number-two man in all the great land of Egypt. As the Pharaoh observed Joseph's discretion, his wisdom, and his enthusiasm, he exclaimed to his servants, "Can we find such a one as this is, a man in whom the Spirit of God is?" (Genesis 1:38).

Each of the great leaders in scripture has been a model for me. Each demonstrated a spirit of enthusiasm, a characteristic I believe is essential for success. A French author, Madame de Staël, has written of enthusiasm that "the sense of this word among the Greeks affords the noblest definition of it; enthusiasm signifies

'God in us.'[2] The joy we feel through having the gospel of Jesus Christ in our lives should translate into great enthusiasm.

I have permitted some of the talks I have given to be published in this book with the hope that I can challenge you to live with greater enthusiasm. It is with the encouragement of my son, Lee, that I finally agreed to have these talks published. He thought the book should be called *Consider Your Ways*. He may be right. I intend the book both as a reminder to consider your ways and as an encouragement to bring more enthusiasm into your life. I am deeply appreciative of Lee's encouragement, editing, and criticism.

NOTES

1. Ralph Waldo Emerson, *The Complete Writings of Ralph Waldo Emerson* (New York: Wm. H. Wise & Co., 1929), pp. 77, 222.

2. Tryon Edwards, Ralph Emerson Browns, et al., *The New Dictionary of Thoughts* (n.p.: Standard Book Co., 1961), p. 176.

LIVING WITH ENTHUSIASM

I HAVE ALWAYS BEEN fascinated by the story of Joseph in the Old Testament. Often I think about the obstacles placed in Joseph's way and how he always seemed to have the spirit and vitality to overcome them.

Joseph began life as the favored son of his father, Jacob. To show his love, Jacob gave Joseph a fine coat of many colors. Jacob had eleven other sons. He did not have twelve coats made—only one, which he gave to Joseph. You can imagine the feeling of Joseph's brothers when he was favored above the rest.

Joseph, of course, made matters worse when he told his brothers about a dream he had one night. Imagine the family sitting at the breakfast table. They are discussing their flocks and grain when Joseph announces, "Oh, by the way, I had a dream last night. We were out in the field and there were twelve shocks of grain. Eleven of them bowed down to the one. Guess who the one was?"

Joseph could not have been popular with his older brothers. In fact, they hated him and could not speak peaceably about him. And Jacob would often compound their resentments when he sent Joseph into the fields to check up on how well his older brothers were tending the flocks.

One day Joseph's older brothers saw him coming from afar and they conspired against him. One said, "Behold, this dreamer cometh. Come now therefore, and let us slay him, and cast him into some pit, and we will say, Some evil beast hath devoured him: and we shall see what will become of his dreams." His older brother, Reuben, persuaded them not to slay Joseph but to cast him into the pit, for then his blood would not be on their hands. But Judah said to his brothers, "What profit is it if we slay our brother, and conceal his blood? Come, and let us sell him to the Ishmeelites, and let not our hand be upon him; for he is our brother and our flesh" (Genesis 37:19–27).

So Joseph was pulled out of the pit and sold to a caravan of Ishmaelites that was on its way to Egypt. What a change in this young man's life! Once favored of his father, he was carried away into a strange land with a strange tongue and a strange religion to be sold as a slave. But Joseph did not become discouraged. He apparently decided that if he had to be sold as a slave, he would present himself the best way he could so perhaps he would be purchased by someone who would give him an opportunity to improve his position in life.

Joseph presented himself so well that the captain of Pharaoh's guard purchased him. In Genesis 39:1–4, we read:

> And Joseph was brought down to Egypt; and Potiphar, an officer of Pharaoh, captain of the guard, an Egyptian, bought him of the hands of the Ishmeelites, which had brought him down thither.
>
> And the Lord was with Joseph, and he was a prosperous man; and he was in the house of his master the Egyptian.
>
> And his master saw that the Lord was with him, and that the Lord made all that he did to prosper in his hand.
>
> And Joseph found grace in his sight, and he served him: and he made him overseer over his house, and all that he had he put into his hand.

So Joseph rose from the status of common slave to be the chief servant in Potiphar's house.

Joseph's enthusiasm and work ethic were soon noticed by everyone in Potiphar's household, including Potiphar's wife. One day Joseph was alone in the house performing his work. Potiphar's wife seized this opportunity and tried to seduce Joseph. She "caught him by his garment," but Joseph ran from her, leaving his garment in her hand (Genesis 39:12).

Later, Potiphar's wife told her husband that Joseph had made inappropriate advances toward her (Genesis 39:17–19). Potiphar was so upset that he had Joseph cast into prison. Again, Joseph, through no fault of his own, was down—but not out.

Joseph refused to become discouraged or depressed. If he had to be a prisoner, he would be the best prisoner in all the prison. His enthusiasm found favor in the sight of the keeper of the prison. He became chief among all the prisoners. This meant Joseph was responsible for all the prisoners in the prison. Once again, he had made the best out of a bad situation.

One day Pharaoh's chief butler and chief baker were cast into the prison that housed Joseph. While they were there, they each had a dream. They were troubled over their dreams and made them known to Joseph, and he interpreted them. According to Joseph's interpretation, the chief butler would be released from prison in three days, and his position would be restored, but the chief baker would be hanged in three days.

Joseph had asked the butler to make mention of him to Pharaoh that he might be brought out of prison to serve him. But when the chief butler was freed from prison, he forgot about Joseph for two years, until Pharaoh had a dream that no one could interpret. Then the butler told Pharaoh that there was a man in prison who could interpret his dreams. Joseph was brought from prison and, of course, he interpreted Pharaoh's dream. Pharaoh immediately recognized Joseph's character. He knew him to be a man of God. He approved Joseph to be over his house. In Genesis we read:

> And the thing was good in the eyes of Pharaoh, and in the eyes of all his servants.
>
> And Pharaoh said unto his servants, Can we find such a one as this is, a man in whom the Spirit of God is?
>
> And Pharaoh said unto Joseph, Forasmuch as God hath shewed thee all this, there is none so discreet and wise as thou art:
>
> Thou shalt be over my house, and according unto thy word shall all my people be ruled: only in the throne will I be greater than thou.

And Pharaoh said unto Joseph, See, I have set thee over all the land of Egypt.

And Pharaoh took off his ring from his hand, and put it upon Joseph's hand, and arrayed him in vestures of fine linen, and put a gold chain about his neck;

And he made him to ride in the second chariot which he had; and they cried before him, Bow the knee: and he made him ruler over all the land of Egypt. (Genesis 41:37–43)

I am sure that the same thing that impresses me about Joseph impresses you. It is the spirit with which he accepted every trial, then turned it to his advantage. He is the exemplar of what Ralph Waldo Emerson meant when he said, "Nothing great was ever achieved without enthusiasm."[1]

In my early years, I developed something of an inferiority complex. After all, I was part of a family in which my brothers and sisters all had great abilities. My older sister had remarkable artistic talent. She was always writing a story or poem that was used in church or in other community gatherings. I determined that since I was her brother, I must possess some artistic talent too. So I analyzed myself and determined that I since I had a strong voice I could become a great singer. I launched a childhood singing career only to discover that although my voice was strong, my range was very limited. In fact, I was a monotone, and the supply of music written in one note is extremely limited. I had to give up my singing career.

My next sister had great athletic ability. She could run faster, hit the ball farther, and catch better than any of the other children on our block. Surely I must have some of her ability, I reasoned. So I stood in front of the mirror and analyzed myself to determine what sport would be most suited to my special athletic abilities. It was obvious. I was taller than most and had average speed. I would become a great basketball player. Once again, I launched a new career. Unfortunately, it was nearly as brief as my singing career. After being hit in the head several times by passes from my teammates, I discovered that my reflexes were too slow to excel at basketball.

My next sister and my brother who was just younger than I were blessed with great minds. They both skipped grades in school, and they still managed to be ranked number one in all their classes. I used to wonder what might happen if they were ever forced to take a class together. Of course, I made no effort to compete with them.

It is interesting to read what my father wrote in his life's history about each of his children. He wrote an entire page about each one of them, reporting their many accomplishments—that is, everyone except me. About me, the only thing my father wrote was "Tom surprised us." That is all the good he could say about me.

Before you feel sorry for me, you should realize that in spite of my lack of talent, I was enthusiastic. I learned from a very early age what an asset my enthusiasm could be. At the dinner table, I complimented my mother so enthusiastically that she consistently gave me the biggest piece of pie. At school, I would raise my hand enthusiastically before my teacher even finished asking a question; fortunately, she would never call on me. As with Joseph, my enthusiasm often helped me turn disadvantages into advantages.

The true test of my enthusiasm came during the years I was an Explorer Scout. The Explorers in our ward had developed quite a reputation for playing volleyball. The year before I became an Explorer, they had gone to the all-Church tournament and placed second.

The year I became eligible to play volleyball, we had another good team. I went to the tryouts and did poorly. My heart was broken, but much to my surprise they selected me for the team anyway. I learned the reason some time later. You see, my father was the bishop of our ward, and the team needed new uniforms. They decided that with the bishop's son on the team, they stood a better chance of receiving new uniforms.

As I sat on the bench that year, I fine-tuned my one talent. I had more enthusiasm than anybody else on the team. I could fire up the players and the crowd while just sitting on the bench. We went all the way to the Church finals and came in second again.

The next year my enthusiasm increased. I even played a little bit. Again, our team went to the all-Church finals, and for the third year in a row we came in second. The fourth year, my final year of playing with the Explorer Scouts, I had the great honor of being elected the team captain. We had lost all of our talented players, and there was not much of a nucleus left. We lost most of our pre-season games. The members of the ward who had given the team such solid support began to stop coming to our games. As the season progressed, however, we began to improve. First we won the stake tournament. Then we won the regional tournament. We surprised our entire ward when we won the area tournament and, for the fourth year in a row, found ourselves in the all-Church finals.

In the first game of the all-Church finals double elimination tournament, surprisingly, we won the consolation championship, which allowed us to come back and compete in the championship bracket. Once again we made it to the final round to play for the Church championship.

We lost the first game 15 to 4. Our coach called me aside between the first and the second games. He reminded me that we didn't have a great deal of talent, but it wasn't talent that won tournaments—it was enthusiasm. He told me to go out on the court and use my enthusiasm to convince my teammates that we could win. My enthusiasm must have helped. We won the second game 15 to 10.

The third game was played very evenly, 1 to 1, 2 to 2, all the way up to 10 to 10. Then one of our players discovered the middle man on the back row couldn't handle his serve, and the score went 11 to 10, 12 to 10, 13 to 10, 14 to 10. We were just one point away from ending a string of second-place finishes and becoming the all-Church champions.

I called time-out and huddled with my teammates. I instructed our server to hit the same spot and we would be Church champions. This time, however, the player on the other team handled the ball. He made an excellent setup to their best player, who pounded a vicious spike over the net. Fortunately, the ball hit one of our players in the chest and bounded off him. I could see the ball was rising to the perfect place and at the perfect angle for my spike. With a short run and a jump, I struck the ball with my fist with all the power I could muster. The ball hit the floor on the other side of the net, and we were the all-Church champions. Enthusiasm had carried us through.

I have never forgotten the lesson of enthusiasm that we learned in winning the all-Church volleyball championship. Someone has written that "enthusiasm is a telescope that advances the misty, distant future into the radiant, tangible present." I believe it. I have found throughout life that my only real talent, the talent of living enthusiastically, has enabled me to accomplish much more than my modest talents would have led anyone to expect. I surprised even my father.

NOTE

1. *The Oxford Dictionary of Quotations,* 2d edition (London: Oxford University Press, 1950), p. 200.

"Serve God Acceptably with Reverence and Godly Fear"

I HAVE BEEN THINKING about reverence. While I believe that reverence is often exhibited through reverent behaviors, this has not been the focus of my thoughts. I have been more concerned about attitude—an attitude of deepest respect and veneration toward Deity. If we can cultivate reverent attitudes among the members of the Church, reverent behaviors will follow.

The scriptures remind us constantly that goodness is centered in the heart. Those who put on an appearance only to receive the honors of men, but have unclean hearts, are called hypocrites. It is not enough to behave reverently; we must feel in our hearts reverence for our Heavenly Father and our Lord, Jesus Christ. Reverence flows from our admiration and respect for Deity. Those who are truly reverent are those who have paid the price to know the glory of the Father and his Son. As Paul admonished, we "serve God acceptably with reverence and godly fear" (Hebrews 12:28).

The story of Alma the Younger provides a wonderful illustration of the reverence we feel in our hearts when we come to know God. As a young man, Alma chose to be sinful and worldly. He was so astonished when an angel appeared to him to call him to repentance that he became mute and so weak that he could not move.

After two days and two nights, when Alma's limbs received their strength, he stood up and began to speak unto the people about how he had been redeemed of the Lord. Alma was born again. He was a new creature. His heart had changed.

In chapter 27 of Mosiah, verse 29, Alma describes his marvelous transformation: "My soul hath been redeemed from the gall of bitterness and bonds of iniquity. I was in the darkest abyss; but now I behold the marvelous light of God. My soul was racked with eternal torment; but I am snatched, and my soul is pained no more."

Then in verse 31, we see evidence of Alma's deep reverence for God: "Yea, every knee shall bow, and every tongue confess before him. Yea, even at the last day, when all men shall stand to be judged of him, then shall they confess that he is God; then shall they confess, who live without God in the world, that the judgment of an everlasting punishment is just upon them; and they shall quake, and tremble, and shrink beneath the glance of his all-searching eye."

Alma's experience had enabled him to understand the glory of God, and also "godly fear." He held the deepest respect and veneration for God. Having seen "the marvelous light of God," he recognized God's power and majesty.

Several years ago I had the opportunity of traveling with the president of the Church to attend a series of area conferences. I will never forget the contrast between two conferences that were held just a few days apart. The first area conference was held in a large arena, and as we sat on the stand we noticed continuous movement by the people. We saw individuals throughout the arena leaning over and whispering to family members and friends seated next to them. Giving the members the benefit of the doubt, we attributed the general lack of reverence to the nature of the facility.

A few days later, we were in another country attending another area conference in an arena much like the first. When we entered the arena, however, an immediate hush came over the congregation. As we sat through the two-hour general session, there was very little movement among the people. Everyone listened intently. Great attention and respect was shown all the speakers, and when the prophet spoke, it was so quiet in the arena that you could have heard a pin drop.

After the meeting was over, I asked the priesthood leaders what they had done to prepare the people for the conference. They told me that their preparations had been simple. They had asked priesthood holders to explain to the members of their families, and also the families they home taught, that at the area conference they would be hearing the words of the prophet and the apostles. The priesthood leaders explained that the reverence their people felt for God and his servants was the basis for their reverent behavior at the conference.

I remember as a young child being taught a valuable lesson by my bishop. President Heber J. Grant had just visited our community to dedicate our new meetinghouse. Our bishop was so impressed with the dedicatory prayer that the next Tuesday when we went to Primary, he attended with us. He wanted to teach us to have respect for the building because it had been dedicated as a place of worship.

The bishop took us on a tour of our new chapel and showed us the various features of the building to impress upon us that it was now a house dedicated to the Lord. First he pointed to the back of the hall, where the beehive emblem had been painted above the back exit doors. He explained that the beehive was the emblem of industry to the early pioneers. "The bees are ever busy bringing honey and sweetness into the hive," he said. The beehive painted on our wall was to be a reminder of the importance of being industrious each day and gathering the good things of this world and bringing them with us to share as we worshipped in Sunday services.

Then he pointed to the large painting on the front wall depicting the arrival of the pioneers into the Salt Lake Valley. He spoke to us about the sacrifices the pioneers had made for us by coming west and building our cities and the first houses of worship so that we could partake of the Spirit of the Lord and be instructed in the Lord's ways.

The bishop directed our attention to two other paintings, one on each side of the large painting of the pioneers. The painting on the right was of the Prophet Joseph Smith, and the one on the left was of President Brigham Young. The bishop spent time telling us about the reverence we should have for the prophets, and he told us we should heed their words of counsel. Then he reminded us of President Grant's trip and described some of the sacrifices he had made in order to come and dedicate this building and commend it to the care and keeping of the Lord.

The bishop explained the motif that ran around the entire chapel. It was of a dart and an egg, repeated over and over again. He discussed why this motif was selected—the egg signifying new life, the dart signifying the end of life. The egg was a reminder of our mortal birth and the time we have on earth to be taught and trained in the ways of the Lord, to be obedient to his will, and to participate in the sacred ordinances that qualify us to return to his presence. The dart represented the time of transition from mortality to immortality. He reminded us that if we proved ourselves worthy, we would be blessed with the greatest gift of God, the gift of eternal life.

Finally, for a special emphasis, the bishop focused our attention on the sacrament table. He instructed us about the purpose of the sacrament, explaining that it was a time to renew our baptismal covenants and to remember the atoning sacrifice of our Lord and Savior. The bishop then concluded with an appeal to each of us to always be reverent in this house, which had been dedicated to the Lord.

Witnessing the dedication of our chapel by a prophet of God and attending the tour guided by my bishop impressed me greatly. I realized that every time I entered the chapel I was entering a holy place. It was not difficult for me to be reverent at church, because all around me there were reminders of the Lord, his servants, and his eternal plan for me. These reminders reinforced my reverent attitude, and reverent behavior followed.

Of course, today's meetinghouses are not constructed with the same design features as the building where I attended church as a boy. However, all Latter-day Saint meetinghouses center on the mission of our Savior. The chapels within these buildings are rooms dedicated for the purpose of worshipping him. Today's bishops may not be able to instruct the Primary as my former bishop did, because our chapels are usually occupied during Primary time. The responsibility to teach children about the chapel as a place of reverence may shift to parents. Perhaps the parents of the Church could find time to be alone with their children in the chapel and explain to them that it is a special place, dedicated to the Lord, wherein only reverent attitudes and behaviors are acceptable.

If reverence is an attitude toward Deity, then it is a private feeling. It is something we feel inside our hearts no matter what is going on around us. It is also a personal responsibility. We cannot blame others for disturbing our reverent attitudes.

Where, then, does developing a reverent attitude begin? The home is the key to reverence, as it is to every other godlike virtue. It is during personal and family prayer that little ones learn how to bow their heads, fold their arms, and close their eyes while our Father in Heaven is being addressed. Reverence is taught when a mother takes time to be certain that during each day there is a quiet period, devoid of the hustle and bustle of daily activities, during which just parents and children have time together in quiet solitude for reflection and teaching.

It is taught during family home evenings, which are a part of our home life, where children are taught that there are special times, not only at church but at home, when we learn of our Heavenly Father and when everyone needs to be on their best behavior. Behavior learned at home determines behavior in church meetings. A child who has learned to pray at home understands that he must be quiet and still during prayers in worship services.

One Sunday my granddaughter Diana, who was four years old at the time, was sitting next to her father at church. Diana sat reverently, enjoying the comfort of her father's arm holding her close to him. When the bishop stood up and announced the sacrament hymn, however, Diana gently lifted her father's arm from her shoulder and placed it in his lap. Then she sat up straight and folded her arms. She looked over at her father and encouraged him to do the same.

Diana's message to her father was perfectly clear. She was telling him to turn his complete and total attention to the Savior. This is the message a reverent attitude always conveys, and when reverent attitudes abound, reverent behaviors flourish. I pray that, like Diana, we may all strive to develop reverent attitudes so we may "serve God acceptably with reverence and godly fear" (Hebrews 12:28).

Let us ever understand the value of our personal example of devotion and respect for him whom we call "Wonderful, Counsellor, The mighty God, The everlasting Father, The Prince of Peace" (Isaiah 9:6). Let us begin with the development of reverent attitudes, then behave reverently as we honor him who is the bread of life.

3

"Train Up a Child"

In Proverbs 22:6, we read, "Train up a child in the way he should go: and when he is old, he will not depart from it."

The Lord has been very specific in his instructions to parents in this day. In the Doctrine and Covenants we read:

> And again, inasmuch as parents have children in Zion, or in any of her stakes which are organized, that teach them not to understand the doctrine of repentance, faith in Christ the Son of the living God, and of baptism and the gift of the Holy Ghost by the laying on of the hands, when eight years old, the sin be upon the heads of the parents. . . .
>
> And they shall also teach their children to pray, and to walk uprightly before the Lord. (D&C 68:25, 28)

The language of this scripture is direct, and it leaves no room for misunderstanding. The responsibility for training children rests squarely on the shoulders of their parents.

Many years ago, I had the great pleasure of serving as second counselor in the Sunday School presidency, with specific responsibility for what was then the Junior Sunday School. Each Sunday I would watch a particular father bring his son to Sunday School. The boy would be crying and screaming, begging not to be turned over to the teacher. I watched the father take him up to his classroom, push him through the door, and then hold the doorknob on the other side so the son could not leave, while inside the classroom the boy's teacher tried to comfort him. It was almost as if the father were saying, "I haven't the patience or the time to train this young man. I am turning him over to you, teacher, to teach him how to be reverent in his Sunday School class."

I had almost the same feeling some time ago when I spent a few hours with the president of Brigham Young University. I had asked for an appointment to discuss with him what the priesthood could do to help students live in accordance with the honor code at BYU. The honor code (which all BYU students agree to follow while attending the university) specifies acceptable and unacceptable behaviors for students at that institution. As I listened to the leader of that great university, I was reminded of my experience in Junior Sunday School many years ago. I had the feeling that many parents were bringing their children to the doorstep of BYU, pushing them through the door, then holding onto the doorknob, expecting the university to assume the responsibility for training up their children.

This same feeling comes to me occasionally when I interview missionaries who are experiencing difficulties in the mission field. Some parents must think, "If only we can send our child on a mission, it will make up for the many years we have neglected to teach him or her the principles of the gospel."

Of course, the large majority of the students entering Brigham Young University, as well as the young men and women serving missions throughout the world, have been trained in good homes. Their conduct is exemplary. However, a small percentage of both students and missionaries leave home with serious unresolved problems, and trends indicate the number is increasing. My message to the parents of these children—and in fact to the parents of all children—is this: the core work of shaping our children's beliefs and character cannot be delegated to an outside source. Parents must take the time and have the patience to ensure in a carefully planned, organized way that the foundation of gospel teachings is laid in their homes.

President Ezra Taft Benson said, "If we continue with present trends, we can expect to have more emotionally disturbed young people, more divorce, more depression, and more suicide. The family is the most effective place to instill lasting values in its members. Where family life is strong and based on principles and practices of the gospel of Jesus Christ, these problems do not as readily appear."[1]

At the time I was a new parent, President David O. McKay presided over the Church. His counsel was clear and direct regarding parents' responsibilities to their children. He taught that the most precious gift a man and woman can receive is a child of God, and that the rearing of a child is basically, fundamentally, and exclusively a spiritual process.

He directed parents on the basic principles needed to teach their children. He emphasized that the first and most important inner quality a parent can instill in a child is faith in God, that the first and most important action a child can learn is obedience, and that the most powerful tool parents have as they teach a child is love.[2] We will examine these three basic principles.

President Brigham Young instructed parents by saying, "If each and every one of us who are parents will reflect upon the responsibilities devolving upon us we shall come to the conclusion that we should never permit ourselves to do anything that we are not willing to see our children do. We should set them an example that we wish them to imitate."[3]

The best way for parents to *instill* faith is to *have* faith. Children must see their parents on their knees daily, asking for God's blessings and expressing their gratitude to him. Children need to see fathers using their priesthood to administer to family members in need of a blessing. They need to see parents reverently worshipping in our sacrament meetings. They need to see parents cheerfully and willingly giving of their time and talents to the building of the Lord's kingdom here on earth. They need to see parents proving their faith by the payment of tithes and offerings. They need to see parents diligently studying and discussing the scriptures to increase their faith and understanding.

Recently I read an article about a study to determine the benefits of reading to children. It stated that when a mother or a father consistently reads to a child, the child performs at a much higher level in the early grades of school. Parents have many options from which to choose when they read to their children. Why not introduce the principles of the gospel through Bible and Book of Mormon stories, stories of latter-day prophets, and stories from family histories? Certainly, if parents will be faithful in teaching gospel ideals to their children, they will deepen the faith of their children.

The second principle President McKay recommended was for our children to learn *obedience.* President Joseph Fielding Smith said:

> Of course there should be prayer and faith and love and obedience to God in the home. It is the duty of parents to teach their children these saving principles of the gospel of Jesus Christ, so that they will know why they are to be baptized and that they may be impressed in their hearts with a desire to continue to keep the commandments of God after they are baptized, that they may come back into his presence. Do you, my good brethren and sisters, want your families, your children; do you want to be sealed to your fathers and your mothers before you . . . ? If so, then you must begin by teaching at the cradle-side. You are to teach by example as well as precept.[4]

I remember one time when I was especially impressed by the need to teach obedience to one of my children. I had just started a new job that required me to work long hours, and I admit I was somewhat neglectful of my family. My son seemed to crave more time and attention from me, and he was showing it by finding all sorts of ways to disobey. One day when I came home, his mother had him prepared to take me downstairs to show me the most recent damage from his mischief. As we descended the stairs, he sheepishly opened the door to our food storage room. There I found he had been practicing his marksmanship on our food storage with his dart set. He caught my attention all right! I realized he was looking to me to set expectations and standards for his behavior. We had a long talk. I laid down the law, but I also committed to be a better father. My son responded as most young children would: he became more obedient.

It is absolutely essential that we teach obedience early in the lives of our children, especially obedience to the commandments of God.

The third principle President McKay taught was the necessity of *love*. I have always been impressed that when the Lord was teaching his disciples at the Last Supper, he served them by washing their feet, and then he taught them about love. He said, "A new commandment I give unto you, That ye love one another; as I have loved you, that ye also love one another" (John 13:34).

I once read a *Reader's Digest* article about enduring values. It stated:

> The climate of our times tends to support the idea that love is like a seasonal monsoon: it comes, it blows fiercely; it goes by. That is too bad, because a child needs the kind of love that is as trustworthy as the rising of the sun. If a child is to grow up to truly join the human race, he needs to know how to keep love alive.
>
> A child should learn not merely to love but to be a loving person, to make love his stance in the world. "Love" may come and go, but a loving person, like the sun itself, never loses his [or her] sustaining warmth.[5]

I challenge the members of the Church to pause, ponder, and think of the value of an immortal soul, especially one entrusted to them as parents. Where are *your* priorities? Have you committed yourself to give necessary and sufficient time to train your children?

Professor Nick Stinnett of the University of Nebraska gave a most interesting talk at an annual meeting of the National Council on Family Relations. He discussed characteristics of strong families. His six points were:

1. A strong family spends a significant amount of time together while playing, working, eating, or engaging in recreation. While family members all had outside interests, they found adequate time to spend together.

2. Strong families have a high degree of commitment to each family member, as indicated not only by the time spent together but also by their ability to work together in a common cause.

3. Strong families have good communication patterns, as indicated by the time spent listening and speaking to each other in conversation.

4. Strong families have a high degree of religious orientation.

5. Because they have spent time together, are committed to each other, and have good communication patterns, strong families have the ability to deal with crises in a positive way.

6. Members of strong families frequently give each other compliments that are genuine and not superficial.[6]

We who have embraced the gospel of Jesus Christ ought to demonstrate the devotion and determination necessary to build strong family units. May God bless us that we may "organize [ourselves]; prepare every needful thing, and establish a house" that will provide the fundamental values of faith, obedience, and love for our children (D&C 109:8). May we train up our children in the ways that they should go, and may they never depart from them (see Proverbs 22:6).

NOTES

1. "Fundamentals of Enduring Family Relationships," *Ensign,* November 1982, p. 59.

2. See David O. McKay, *Gospel Ideals* (Salt Lake City: Deseret News Press, 1954), pp. 481–84, 487–88.

3. Brigham Young, in *Journal of Discourses,* 26 vols. (London: Latter-day Saints' Book Depot, 1854–86), 14:192. Hereafter cited as *Journal of Discourses.*

4. Official Report of the One Hundred Nineteenth Semiannual Conference of The Church of Jesus Christ of Latter-day Saints, October 1, 2, and 3, 1948 (Salt Lake City: The Church of Jesus Christ of Latter-day Saints, 1948), p. 153. Hereafter cited as Conference Report, followed by month and year of report.

5. *Reader's Digest,* June 1981, p. 164.

6. See "In Search of Strong Families, " in *Building Family Strengths: Blueprints for Action,* ed. Nick Stinnett et al. (Lincoln: University of Nebraska Press, 1979), pp. 23–30.

4

"IF YE ARE
PREPARED YE SHALL NOT FEAR"

LEHI HAD A marvelous dream while he journeyed with his family in the wilderness. This dream or vision of the tree of life, which was presented symbolically, provides us with much knowledge about life and the course we should be following. The scriptures record:

> And it came to pass that I beheld a tree, whose fruit was desirable to make one happy.
>
> And it came to pass that I did go forth and partake of the fruit thereof; and I beheld that it was most sweet, above all that I ever before tasted. Yea, and I beheld that the fruit thereof was white, to exceed all the whiteness that I had ever seen.
>
> And as I partook of the fruit thereof it filled my soul with exceedingly great joy; wherefore, I began to be desirous that my family should partake of it also; for I knew that it was desirable above all other fruit. (1 Nephi 8:10–12)

In Lehi's dream, he beheld many seeking to come forward to partake of this delicious fruit, which was defined as the love of God. A rod of iron, meaning the word of God, would lead them to the tree. However, along the path there was also a mist of darkness, or temptations, that caused many to become lost along the way. Again the scriptures record:

> And it came to pass that I beheld others pressing forward, and they came forth and caught hold of the end of the rod of iron; and they did press forward through the mist of darkness,

clinging to the rod of iron, even until they did come forth and partake of the fruit of the tree.

And after they had partaken of the fruit of the tree they did cast their eyes about as if they were ashamed.

And I also cast my eyes round about, and beheld, on the other side of the river of water, a great and spacious building; and it stood as it were in the air, high above the earth.

And it was filled with people, both old and young, both male and female; and their manner of dress was exceedingly fine; and they were in the attitude of mocking and pointing their fingers towards those who had come at and were partaking of the fruit.

And after they had tasted of the fruit they were ashamed, because of those that were scoffing at them; and they fell away into forbidden paths and were lost. (1 Nephi 8:24–28)

This is the part of Lehi's dream on which I would like to focus. The current cries we hear coming from the great and spacious building tempt us to compete for ownership of the things of this world. We think we need a larger home with a three-car garage, a recreational vehicle parked next to it. We long for designer clothes, extra TV sets (all with VCRs), the latest-model computers, and the newest car. We think we must involve our children in costly activities such as athletic camps and similarly expensive programs. Often these items are purchased with borrowed money and without any thought of providing for our future needs. The results of all of this instant gratification are overloaded bankruptcy courts and families that are far too preoccupied with their financial burdens.

We live in a most exciting and challenging period of human history. As technology sweeps through every facet of life, changes are occurring so rapidly that it can be difficult for us to keep our lives in balance. To maintain some semblance of stability in our lives, it is essential that we plan for our future. I believe it is time to review (perhaps with some urgency) the counsel we have received regarding our personal and family preparedness. We want to be found with oil in our lamps sufficient to endure to the end. President Spencer W. Kimball admonished us that we cannot place sufficient oil in our preparedness lamps by simply avoiding evil.

We must also be anxiously engaged in a positive program of preparation—a program based on living the gospel. President Kimball said, "In our lives the oil of preparedness is accumulated drop by drop in righteous living."[1] He also issued a warning: "The Lord will not translate one's good hopes and desires and intentions into works. Each of us must do that for himself."[2]

On a daily basis we witness widely fluctuating inflation, wars, interpersonal conflicts, national disasters, variances in weather conditions, innumerable forces of immorality, crime, and violence, attacks and pressures on families and individuals, technological advances that make occupations obsolete, and so on. The need for preparation is abundantly clear. The great blessing of being prepared gives us freedom from fear, as guaranteed to us by the Lord: "If ye are prepared ye shall not fear" (D&C 38:30).

Just as it is important to prepare ourselves spiritually, we must also prepare for our temporal needs. We all need to take the time to ask ourselves, What preparations should we make to care for our needs and the needs of our families?

We have been instructed for years to follow at least four requirements in preparing for that which is to come.

First, gain an adequate education. Learn a trade or profession to enable you to obtain steady employment that will provide remuneration sufficient to care for yourself and your family. The rapidly changing world breeds obsolescence and requires us to be continually engaged in preparing ourselves for the future. We can become antiquated in our professions if we do not make the effort to stay up-to-date. Imagine how many patients a dentist would have if he continued to use the same tools and techniques he used a decade ago. What about a businessman who tried to compete without the use of computers? Or a builder who had not stayed abreast of the new materials and methods available? Education has, of necessity, become a lifelong pursuit. We must allot sufficient time in our schedules to educate ourselves for now and for the future.

Second, live strictly within your income and save something for a rainy day. Incorporate in your lives the discipline of budgeting what the Lord has blessed you with. As regularly as you pay your tithing, set aside an amount needed for future family requirements. Include your children while planning for the future. I am convinced that in many backyards, a crop of corn, raspberries, or tomatoes, planted and harvested by your children each year and sold to your neighbors, will in time yield enough to make a major contribution to a missionary or a college education fund. Go out in your garage and look over all the *unused* bicycles, toy cars, athletic equipment, skis, roller blades, and so forth, and calculate what the return would have been had the costs of these items been invested in future needs. Remember, I emphasized *unused* articles. How many of you have seen garages so full of things there is no longer room for the car?

Third, avoid excessive debt. Necessary debt should be incurred only after careful, thoughtful prayer and after obtaining the best possible advice. We need the discipline to stay well within our ability to pay. Wisely we have been counseled to avoid debt as we would avoid the plague. President J. Reuben Clark fearlessly and repeatedly counseled the members of the Church to take action: "Live within your means. Get out of debt. Keep out of debt. Lay by for a rainy day which has always come and will come again. Practice and increase your habits of thrift, industry, economy, frugality."[3]

We should all display in a prominent place President Clark's description of interest: "Interest never sleeps nor sickens nor dies. . . . Once in debt, interest is your companion every minute of the day and night; you cannot shun it or slip away from it; you cannot dismiss it; it yields neither to entreaties, demands, or orders; and whenever you get in its way or cross its course or fail to meet its demands, it crushes you."[4]

The incurring of debt is such an enticement. Accompanying the ease with which we can obtain debt should be the great caution of avoidance. Take the opportunity to compute how much you will add to your personal net worth if your home mortgage is for ten or fifteen years instead of thirty. Compute the value of sweat equity, in which your time and your talents are invested in adding to the size and comfort of your home.

It is so easy to allow consumer debt to get out of hand. If you do not have the discipline to control the use of credit cards, it is better not to have them. A well-managed family does not pay interest—it earns it.

Fourth, acquire and store a reserve of food and supplies that will sustain life. Obtain clothing and build a savings account on a sensible, well-planned basis that can serve well in times of emergency. As long as I can remember, we have been taught to prepare for the future and obtain a year's supply of necessities. I would guess that the years of plenty have almost universally caused us to set aside this counsel. I believe the time to disregard these instructions is over. With the events in the world today, this counsel must be considered with all seriousness.

Careers are ever changing. As young people enter the work force today, many will have major career changes three or four times during their work life. Job changes will occur even more frequently, even ten to twelve times during a person's lifetime work cycle. I know of no other way to prepare for these times of adjustment than to be certain that during times of employment, preparations are being made for less prosperous times, should they occur. Start now to create a plan if you don't already have one, or update your present plan. Watch for best buys that will fit into your year's supply. We are not in a situation that requires panic buying, but we do need a careful plan for purchasing and rotating items in storage. The instability in the world today makes it imperative that we heed this counsel and prepare for the future.

President Harold B. Lee, in commenting about Lehi's great vision, said this: "If there is any one thing most needed in this time of tumult and frustration, when men and women and youth and young adults are desperately seeking for answers to the problems which afflict mankind, it is an 'iron rod' as a safe guide along the straight path on the way to eternal life, amidst the strange and devious roadways that would eventually lead to destruction and to the ruin of all that is 'virtuous, lovely, or of good report.'"[5]

Unfortunately, there are too many among us who are like the scoffers in Lehi's vision. They stand aloof and are inclined to hold in derision the faithful who choose to accept Church authorities as God's special witnesses of the gospel and his agents in directing the affairs of the Church. My sincere counsel to you is to remember the good basic principles we have been taught from the very beginning—the principles of thrift, industry, and integrity that have served mankind seemingly in every period of time. Avoid the great and spacious building that is the pride of the world, for it will fall, and great will be the fall thereof.

May God bless us with the wisdom to follow the counsel we have received as we prepare spiritually and temporally for the strength and security of our family units.

NOTES

1. Spencer W. Kimball, *Faith Precedes the Miracle* (Salt Lake City: Deseret Book Co., 1972), p. 256.

2. Spencer W. Kimball, *The Miracle of Forgiveness* (Salt Lake City: Bookcraft, 1969), p. 8.

3. Conference Report, October 1937, p. 107.

4. Conference Report, April 1938, p. 103.

5. Harold B. Lee, "The Iron Rod," *Ensign,* June 1971, p. 7.

BACK TO GOSPEL BASICS

That they themselves may be prepared, and that my people
may be taught more perfectly, and have experience, and know more
perfectly concerning their duty, and the things which I require at
their hands.

— D & C 1 0 5 : 1 0

UNTIL RECENTLY, part of my assignment included the country of
Peru, an area of the world that is experiencing great turmoil.
Inflation and internal strife have been robbing the Peruvian people
of almost any hope of stability in their lives.

It has been difficult for the General Authorities to visit Peru
regularly because of the dangers of traveling there. Therefore, it
has been necessary for the Peruvian members to assume much
more responsibility for priesthood and auxiliary leadership and
for full-time missionary service.

The area presidency that oversees Peru recognized the need to
fortify the members of the Church there, and after much prayer
and fasting, they decided to emphasize just two basic teachings of
the gospel. They prepared a letter to be delivered to every Peruvian
family. The theme of their letter, in which they stressed family
prayers and family scripture study, was "Being Converted to the
Lord."

The area presidency taught these principles to stake presiden-
cies, who, in turn, instructed their high councils and bishops. The
bishops then instructed ward members, and the home teachers

delivered to each family unit a follow-up letter in which family heads were encouraged to lead their families in daily prayer and scripture study.

The blessings that have come to the Peruvian Saints from daily prayer and scripture study have been most remarkable. It soon became evident that faith and testimony were increasing among members of the Church there. There has been a significant increase in sacrament meeting attendance, which has resulted in a greater sense of community and increased interest among the Saints in loving and caring for each other. Though travel to the temple has become increasingly difficult and dangerous, surprisingly, temple attendance has increased significantly.

The number of Peruvian full-time missionaries immediately began to increase. Now the seven missions in Peru fill nearly all their full-time missionary needs with native Peruvians, and they send missionaries out to serve in other nations as well. Full-time missionaries are arriving in the field better prepared to serve, which, of course, has resulted in an increase in convert baptisms.

A renewed emphasis on two basic gospel practices—daily prayer and scripture study—created a dramatic change and offered increased spirituality and works among the Saints.

The success of the Peruvian Saints should teach all of us the importance of adhering to the basics of a gospel-centered life. Let us consider again the blessings promised us if we faithfully practice daily family prayer and daily family scripture study.

The scriptures are filled with admonitions to stay close to the Lord and call upon his holy name in prayer. In the latter days of the ministry of Alma the Younger, he instructed his sons on how they should live. After Alma's remarkable conversion, he spent his life proclaiming the gospel and perfecting the Saints. Before he died, he wanted to instill in his sons a desire to be obedient to God's will. To Helaman he said:

> O, remember, my son, and learn wisdom in thy youth; yea, learn in thy youth to keep the commandments of God.
>
> Yea, and cry unto God for all thy support; yea, let all thy doings be unto the Lord, and whithersoever thou goest let it be

in the Lord; yea, let all thy thoughts be directed unto the Lord; yea, let the affections of thy heart be placed upon the Lord forever.

Counsel with the Lord in all thy doings, and he will direct thee for good; yea, when thou liest down at night lie down unto the Lord, that he may watch over you in your sleep; and when thou risest in the morning let thy heart be full of thanks unto God; and if ye do these things, ye shall be lifted up at the last day. (Alma 37:35–37)

Prayer is the primary means of communication between God and man. Prayer is an important part of practically every religion, whether it be Christian or otherwise. The Prophet Joseph Smith, speaking on the subject of prayer, stated, "Seek to know God in your closets, call upon him in the fields. Follow the directions of the Book of Mormon, and pray over, and for your families, your cattle, your flocks, your herds, your corn, and all things that you possess; ask the blessing of God upon all your labors, and everything that you engage in."[1]

When we pray to the Lord, we should remember who we are addressing and be prepared to give him our undivided attention as we humbly supplicate him. President John Taylor counseled us this way: "Do you have prayers in your family? . . . And when you do, do you go through the operation like the grinding of a piece of machinery, or do you bow in meekness and with a sincere desire to seek the blessing of God upon you and your household? That is the way that we ought to do, and cultivate a spirit of devotion and trust in God, dedicating ourselves to him, and seeking his blessings."[2]

As parents, it is clearly our duty to teach our children to pray. Regular family prayers establish patterns that bless future generations. It is good to use the sacred pronouns of the scriptures, *thee, thou, thy,* and *thine,* when addressing Deity in prayer, instead of the more common pronouns *you, your,* and *yours.* By so doing, we show greater respect for our Heavenly Father.

It is so satisfying to know that God is mindful of us and ready to respond when we place our trust in him. Why should men and women fear when they humble themselves in seeking divine guidance from the Almighty through frequent and consistent prayer? Though difficulties may arise and reverses may come, in our prayers we can find reassurance as the Lord speaks peace to our souls.

On several occasions President Benson shared the poem "Prayer," by Eliza M. Hickok, with the members of the Church. It is a poem he learned while he was in the Aaronic Priesthood:

> *I know not by what methods rare,*
> *But this I know, God answers prayer.*
> *I know that He has given His Word,*
> *Which tells me prayer is always heard,*
> *And will be answered, soon or late.*
> *And so I pray and calmly wait.*
> *I know not if the blessing sought*
> *Will come in just the way I thought;*
> *But leave my prayers with him alone,*
> *Whose will is wiser than my own,*
> *Assured that He will grant my quest,*
> *Or send some answer far more blest.*[3]

Among the Peruvian Saints, who live in a nation racked with heartache and despair, there has emerged a stronger faith and devotion to our Father in Heaven because they heeded the counsel of his servants to hold daily family prayer. And a special maturing in the gospel has developed among the members of the Church in Peru because they added to their daily family prayers the practice of having daily family scripture study. When the revealed words of the prophets found their way into the hearts of the Saints, these words of counsel brought about a mighty change in the way the people lived and believed. Questions, personal problems, and important concerns were resolved for them by the inspired counsel of the scriptures.

All the standard works of the Church instruct us to read and ponder the scriptures. From the Old Testament we read, "Seek ye out of the book of the Lord, and read" (Isaiah 34:16). From the New Testament, "Search the scriptures; for in them ye think ye have eternal life: and they are they which testify of me" (John

5:39). Nephi, in the Book of Mormon, observes, "My soul delighteth in the scriptures, and my heart pondereth them, and writeth them for the learning and the profit of my children" (2 Nephi 4:15). Counsel from the Pearl of Great Price promises, "And whoso treasureth up my word, shall not be deceived" (Joseph Smith—Matthew 1:37). And finally, in the Doctrine and Covenants we read, "First seek to obtain my word . . . ; study my word which hath gone forth among the children of men" (D&C 11:21–22).

The scriptures are some of our greatest treasures. They contain the Lord's instructions to his people from the beginning of time. In a world so full of the doctrines of men, we are grateful to have the sure anchor of the scriptures to secure our faith. Of the Book of Mormon, President Marion G. Romney said:

> If our young folks are traditioned in the teachings of the Book of Mormon, they will not only be inspired with righteous courage to choose the right by the example of Nephi, the "two thousand sons of Helaman, " and other great characters of the book, they will also be so schooled in the principles of the gospel of Jesus Christ that they will know what is right.
>
> From almost every page of the book, there will come to them a moving testimony that Jesus is indeed the Christ, the Son of the Living God, our Redeemer and Savior. This witness alone will be a sustaining anchor in every storm.[4]

In the Lord's instructions to his children, we find sublime consistency. What the Lord has declared to be right will always be right. What he has declared to be true will always be true. What he has declared to be sinful will always be sinful. Rest assured that when the so-called "enlightened" doctrines of men contradict the holy scriptures, these doctrines of the world bring only heartache, disappointment, and destruction to the souls of mankind.

President Benson counseled us concerning searching the scriptures: "Let us not treat lightly the great things we have received from the hand of the Lord! His word is one of the most valuable gifts He has given us. I urge you to recommit yourselves to a study of the scriptures. Immerse yourselves in them daily. . . .

Read them in your families and teach your children to love and treasure them. Then prayerfully and in counsel with others, seek every way possible to encourage the members of the Church to follow your example."[5]

My counsel to all members of this worldwide church is to recommit yourselves to these two basic practices that have been the source of so many blessings for the Saints in Peru. Never let a day go by without holding family prayer and family scripture study. Put this, the Lord's program, to the test, and see if it does not bless your home with greater peace, hope, love, and faith.

I promise you that daily family prayer and scripture study will build within the walls of your home a security and bonding that will enrich your lives and prepare your families to meet the challenges of today and the eternities to come.

May God grant unto us the desire to seek him reverently and humbly in prayer and in the earnest and sincere study of his word, as contained in his holy scriptures.

NOTES

1. Joseph Smith, *History of The Church of Jesus Christ of Latter-day Saints*, 7 vols., 2d ed. rev., ed. B. H. Roberts (Salt Lake City: The Church of Jesus Christ of Latter-day Saints, 1932–51), 5:31.

2. John Taylor, in *Journal of Discourses*, 21:118.

3. Eliza M. Hickok, "Prayer," *The Best Loved Religious Poems*, ed. James Gilchrist Lawson (New York: Fleming H. Revell Co., 1933), p. 160.

4. Conference Report, April 1960, p. 112.

5. Ezra Taft Benson, "The Power of the Word," *Ensign*, May 1986, p. 82.

6

"Be Familiar with All and Free with Your Substance"

THE BOOK OF MORMON, that great and ancient record of the Nephite nation, offers us the special perspective that comes only from studying what is roughly one thousand years of human history. We see the cycles of nations as they turn to and then away from righteousness. We see the unity that comes from a faith in God and a desire to build his kingdom. And we see the dissension that results when the hearts of the people turn to selfish wants and desires, to the pleasures of the flesh, to riches and worldly possessions.

One of the first warnings from a prophet to the ancient American people is found in the second chapter of Jacob. Jacob denounces his people's love of riches and the pride that has found a place in their hearts. He implores them to turn their hearts again to the Lord:

> The hand of providence hath smiled upon you most pleasingly, that you have obtained many riches; and because some of you have obtained more abundantly than that of your brethren ye are lifted up in the pride of your hearts, and wear stiff necks and high heads because of the costliness of your apparel, and persecute your brethren because ye suppose that ye are better than they.
>
> And now, my brethren, do ye suppose that God justifieth you in this thing? Behold, I say unto you, Nay. But he condemneth you, and if ye persist in these things his judgments must speedily come unto you. (Jacob 2:13–14)

Often the turning away from the Lord described in these verses of scripture accompanies prosperity. Those who are more prosperous become filled with pride, and they look down on their brothers and sisters who have less, thinking them inferior. Although Jacob does not say it, this process can also work the other way. Those who are less fortunate begin to feel deprived. They become consumed by what they do not have, blaming others for their predicament. Often, they will also blame the Lord, and turn their hearts away from him.

The important point to remember is this: the Lord is displeased with preoccupation with worldly possessions, for more often than not the result is a lack of occupation with building his kingdom. This undesired outcome is as likely to result from having too little as too much.

Jacob counsels further, "Think of your brethren like unto yourselves, and be familiar with all and free with your substance, that they may be rich like unto you" (Jacob 2:17).

What we see in this scripture is a direct application of the second great commandment to love our neighbors as ourselves. Jacob tells his people not to discriminate against their brothers and sisters who have less than they do but to share what they have with them. He continues:

> But before ye seek for riches, seek ye for the kingdom of God.
> And after ye have obtained a hope in Christ ye shall obtain riches, if ye seek them; and ye will seek them for the intent to do good—to clothe the naked, and to feed the hungry, and to liberate the captive, and administer relief to the sick and the afflicted. (Jacob 2:18–19)

Often it is the order of things that is fundamental in the Lord's instructions to us. The Lord is not telling us that we should not be prosperous. This would be inconsistent with the many records we have of his blessing his people with prosperity. But he is telling us that we should seek prosperity only after we have sought and found him. Then, because our hearts are right, because we love him first and foremost, we will choose to invest the riches we obtain in building his kingdom.

As we have been told by our prophets, one of the important reasons the Book of Mormon record was kept and, through miraculous circumstances, placed into the hands of Joseph Smith to be translated was to serve as a warning to the people of this generation. Accordingly, we need to take Jacob's counsel to his people to heart. We should read this scripture as though it were written expressly for us in these days, because it was. His words should cause us to ask soul-searching questions of ourselves. Is the order of things right in our own lives? Are we investing, first and foremost, in things that are eternal in nature? Do we have an eternal perspective? Or have we fallen into the trap of investing in the things of this world first, and then forgetting the Lord?

These are difficult questions to answer. Let me propose a simple tool to direct our thinking. Many businesses will measure their activities against those of businesses considered to be the best in their class. These comparisons set a standard that, while difficult to attain, inspires continuous striving and improvement. In a similar manner, stories of the early leaders of the Church have always been helpful to me as examples of what it means to place the kingdom of God first. Perhaps the characters in these stories are the people against whose lives we should measure our own.

The stories of our early Church leaders really began to live for me when I was a young missionary. In those days, missionaries were not blessed with the many teaching aids that we have today. We had our scriptures and a big, black box that contained a record player and a set of records entitled "The Fulness of Times." These records presented an account of the early history of the Church from the First Vision to the Nauvoo period.

There was one episode depicted on the records that would always bring tears to my eyes as my companions and I listened to it. It was the account of Brigham Young and Heber C. Kimball, who left their wives, children, and humble homes to journey to Great Britain in response to their calls to serve in that faraway land. Elder Orson F. Whitney quotes Heber C. Kimball's record of the event:

> "September 14th, " says Heber, "President Brigham Young left his home at Montrose to start on the mission to England. He was so sick that he was unable to go to the Mississippi, a distance of thirty rods, without assistance. After he had crossed the river he rode behind Israel Barlow on his horse to my house, where he continued sick until the 18th. He left his wife sick with a babe only three weeks old, and all his other children were sick and unable to wait upon each other. Not one soul of them was able to go to the well for a pail of water, and they were without a second suit to their backs, for the mob in Missouri had taken nearly all he had. On the 17th, Sister Mary Ann Young got a boy to carry her up in his wagon to my house, that she might nurse and comfort Brother Brigham to the hour of starting.
>
> "September 18th, Charles Hubbard sent his boy with a wagon and span of horses to my house; our trunks were put into the wagon by some brethren; I went to my bed and shook hands with my wife who was then shaking with a chill, having two children lying sick by her side; I embraced her and my children, and bade them farewell. My only well child was little Heber P., and it was with difficulty he could carry a couple of quarts of water at a time, to assist in quenching their thirst.
>
> "It was with difficulty we got into the wagon, and started down the hill about ten rods; it appeared to me as though my very inmost parts would melt within me at leaving my family in such a condition, as it were almost in the arms of death. I felt as though I could not endure it. I asked the teamster to stop, and said to Brother Brigham, 'This is pretty tough, isn't it; let's rise up and give them a cheer.' We arose, and swinging our hats three times over our heads, shouted: 'Hurrah, hurrah for Israel.' Vilate, hearing the noise, arose from her bed and came to the door. She had a smile on her face. Vilate and Mary Ann Young cried out to us: 'Goodbye, God bless you.' We returned the compliment, and then told the driver to go ahead. After this I felt a spirit of joy and gratitude, having had the satisfaction of seeing my wife standing upon her feet, instead of leaving her in bed, knowing well that I should not see them again for two or three years."[1]

I have often wondered how these brethren, as valiant as they were, could do what they did. Truly they were willing to make any sacrifice asked of them to build the kingdom of God. Truly they were laying up "treasures in heaven, where neither moth nor rust doth corrupt" (Matthew 6:20).

There is something else about this story, however, that has always intrigued me. As Brigham Young and Heber C. Kimball left on their missions to Great Britain, there appeared to be a lot of support from their brethren to help them on their way. Israel Barlow assisted Brigham Young as he traveled to Heber Kimball's house. Several days later, Charles Hubbard sent his son with a wagon to the Kimball home to assist the two missionaries as they began their long journey. Many other good Saints assisted them, offering food and housing, medical care, transportation, and even cash donations.

If we look carefully at this story, we catch a glimpse of the unity that must have existed among the Saints in those early days. As husbands and fathers would leave for missionary service, their departure was made easier because they knew that brothers, sisters, priesthood leaders, and friends would step in to help fill the void created by their absence. These brethren were able to invest in building the kingdom of God in faraway lands because they knew that others would be investing in building the kingdom at home, by offering their loved ones whatever assistance was needed. There was a unique bonding, a special faith in the community of Saints, who were dedicated to a common goal, a common purpose. If we return to Jacob's counsel to his people, we see the same message communicated as he instructs them to be familiar with all and to share freely of their substance (see Jacob 2:17).

What this suggests to me is that if we look at how we treat our brothers and sisters in the Church, we can tell whether or not we put the kingdom of God first. Is there a special bond uniting us? Is there an absence of envy and backbiting? Do we rejoice in the success of a brother or sister as much as our own? Do we share of our substance so all may be rich like unto us? Ultimately, are we our brothers' and sisters' keepers?

As I travel throughout the Church I marvel at all the positive things that are occurring, yet I never feel that we, as a people, are living up to all of our potential. My sense is that we do not always work together, that we are still too much consumed by personal aspirations for the honors of men, and that we show too little interest in the common goal of building the Lord's kingdom.

When we look at all the Lord asks of us, it can sometimes seem overwhelming. Of course, where much has been given, much is expected. I believe it is helpful when faced with an enormous challenge to view it as a step-by-step process. We begin by taking the first step, then continue by taking one step at a time. I am certain that the Lord is pleased even with our small beginnings, because in his infinite wisdom he knows that small things often become great things.

The first step is for us to deepen our commitment to the Lord and his glorious work. Again, this is a commitment to place his work first in our hearts and minds. Our subsequent steps are guided by this initial commitment but can, of course, take several directions.

We can help by serving our brothers and sisters in the Church. We can go to those who have not yet received the gospel and convert them to its truth. We can go to the temple and perform this same redeeming work for the dead. As we engage in the work of the Lord, he will increase our capacity as we increase our desire. We will pull closer together as a people engaged in a common effort. Through sacrifices we make for one another and for God, we will realize our potential as Heavenly Father's children and prepare the way for the eventual, glorious return of the Savior.

May each of us accept this challenge to seek the kingdom of God before and above anything else, and by so doing may we draw closer together as a people until we are of one heart and one mind.

NOTE

1. Orson F. Whitney, *Life of Heber C. Kimball* (Salt Lake City: Bookcraft, 1945), pp. 265–66.

"Consider Your Ways"

Some time ago, I read an article that addressed the question of differences in wealth among various nations. The article's author asked why certain nations succeed at developing wealth-creating economies while others fail. This is a complex question, and no single answer can explain everything; but according to the article, a lot can be explained by differences in national cultures. The countries that are successful at creating wealth stress education, freedom, delayed gratification, mutual trust, and hard work.

Let me posit an alternative hypothesis: The success of a nation depends on its people's knowledge of God and their obedience to his commandments. The relationship is as simple and straightforward as the Lord's words to Joseph Smith: "I, the Lord, am bound when ye do what I say; but when ye do not what I say, ye have no promise" (D&C 82:10).

There is a strong correlation between the success of nations and their knowledge and obedience to God's commandments. His commandments stress education (see D&C 88:118); freedom and agency (see D&C 58:28); delayed gratification and an emphasis on matters of eternal, not worldly, value (see Matthew 6:19–21; Luke 16:20–31); trust in the Lord (see 2 Nephi 4:34); and hard work (Moroni 9:6).

In the first chapter of Haggai, we read:

> Now therefore thus saith the Lord of hosts; Consider your ways.
> Ye have sown much, and bring in little; ye eat, but ye have

not enough; ye drink, but ye are not filled with drink; ye clothe you, but there is none warm; and he that earneth wages earneth wages to put it into a bag with holes.

Thus saith the Lord of hosts; Consider your ways. (Haggai 1:5–7)

The context of these verses of scripture is interesting. The people of Israel were delaying the construction of the temple of Zerubbabel. The Lord spoke through his prophet, Haggai, and warned the people to reorder their priorities and build the temple. When he told the people to consider their ways, he reminded them that blessings are not entitlements but rather are contingent on obedience to his word. He threatened to withhold his blessings unless the people commenced work on his house. Fortunately, the people did consider their ways, and "they came and did work in the house of the Lord of hosts, their God" (Haggai 1:14).

Will Durant, the noted historian, summarized the reasons for the fall of the Roman Empire as follows:

1. The breakdown of the family and rapid increase of divorce.

2. The spiraling rise of taxes and extravagant spending.

3. The mounting craze for pleasure and the brutalization of sports.

4. The decay of religion into many confused forms of worship, leaving the people without a uniform guide.[1]

In other words, the fall of the Roman Empire resulted from breakdowns of the nuclear family, of financial discipline, of morality, and of religious traditions.

Are we not simply repeating history? While these problems may manifest themselves in different ways, they are as prevalent today as they were at the time immediately preceding the fall of Rome. Moreover, they all represent direct violations of God's commandments. Isn't it time that we consider our ways? Shouldn't we contemplate our roles as spouses and parents, battle the worldliness and immorality that surrounds us, and work to deepen our religious beliefs?

Consider your family. Among the first instructions given to man and woman was this injunction: "Therefore shall a man leave his father and his mother, and shall cleave unto his wife: and they shall be one flesh" (Genesis 2:24).

God, in his divine plan, ordained marriage to bring about his basic organizational unit, the family. The roles of husband and wife were clearly defined from the beginning. In the Lord's plan, these roles are unchanged and eternal.

The Lord has given to men the responsibility to be providers and protectors. If the Lord's plan is to work, men must learn how to perform the leadership role he has designed for them. Husbands, could I remind you of some of your leadership requirements?

First, the Lord's warnings about the practice of "unrighteous dominion" (see D&C 121:39–44) apply equally as well to husbands as to Church leaders. Your wives are not your subordinates. They are not your counselors. They are your eternal companions and equals. Always remember, the presidency of an eternal family is a shared presidency.

Second, in most cases, a husband should be the primary provider for the family. Often, sacrifice is required of husbands to prepare themselves to provide adequately for their families. Moreover, husbands should assist members of their families in distinguishing between wants and basic needs. Families do not need everything they want. Often, the unchecked fulfillment of wants places unnecessary financial burdens on families.

Third, husbands have a twenty-four-hour-a-day job showing appreciation and consideration for their wives. A prophet has said of womanhood, "A beautiful, modest, gracious woman is creation's masterpiece."[2] A husband has the responsibility to safeguard this masterpiece, who is his wife.

The examples of our most recent prophets—from President McKay to President Hinckley—define the way husbands should treat their wives. A righteous husband's greatest concern should be his wife's happiness.

Second only in importance to being an eternal companion is being an eternal parent. Fathers and mothers, consider your ways.

My children taught me a great lesson many years ago. Our family had just moved from California to New York City, where I had accepted a position with a new company. We began the process of finding a new home by looking in the communities closest to the city. Gradually, however, we moved farther away from the city to find a home and neighborhood more suited to our needs. In New Canaan, Connecticut, we found our dream home. It was a beautiful one-story house nestled in the lovely, dark, and deep woods of New England.

The final test before purchasing the home was for me to ride the commuter train to New York City to check how long it took. I made the trip and returned quite discouraged. The trip was one and a half hours each way. I returned to the motel where my family was waiting for me and presented my children with a choice. "You can either have this new home or a father," I said.

Much to my surprise, they responded, "We'll take the home. You're never around anyway."

I was devastated. If what they were telling me was true, I needed to repent fast. My children needed a father who was home more. Eventually, we reached a compromise. We bought a home in Scarsdale, New York, a community only a forty-five-minute train ride from New York City. I stopped working on Saturdays and began to take more seriously my role as father.

President David O. McKay said, "I have but one thought in my heart for the young folk of the Church, and that is that they be happy. I know of no other place than home where more happiness can be found in this life. It is possible to make home a bit of heaven; indeed, I picture heaven to be a continuation of the ideal home."[3]

When I considered my ways, these words of a prophet penetrated my very soul. Creating the ideal home described by President McKay became my goal as a husband and father.

Consider how much time you spend in pursuit of material possessions. Our uncontrolled appetites and consuming drive for material gain are sending our nation on a downward spiral, and many members of the Church are going along for the ride. What has happened to the values of thrift, industry, economy, and frugality? When was delayed gratification displaced by instant gratification? One writer has noted that in the 1950s people were interested in exporting and investing; in the 1990s they are interested in importing and in leveraging credit to enhance their speculative capacity.

In Lehi's dream, the great and spacious building represented "the pride of the world" (1 Nephi 11:36). The current cries we hear coming from the great and spacious building tempt the Saints to base their self-esteem on how many material possessions they own. We think we need a larger home with at least a three-car garage. We want a boat and a large recreational vehicle to pull it. We set our hearts on designer clothing, multiple televisions and VCRs, the latest model computers, and the newest car. We think that our children's summers would be empty without cheerleader and basketball camps. Often, we borrow money to provide these so-called "necessities." The result of this all-too-instant gratification is overloaded bankruptcy courts and two-career families. Consider your ways.

President J. Reuben Clark fearlessly and repeatedly counseled the members of the Church to avoid unnecessary debt. He said, "Once in debt, interest is your companion every minute of the day and night; you cannot shun it or slip away from it; you cannot dismiss it; it yields neither to entreaties, demands, or orders; and whenever you get in its way or cross its course or fail to meet its demands, it crushes you."[4]

Remember Jacob's instructions to his people to seek the kingdom of God before they sought riches. Then, if riches were obtained, the money would be put to use in building the kingdom of God (see Jacob 2:18–19).

Elder James E. Talmage taught the Saints this about material possessions: "Material belongings, relative wealth or poverty, physical environment—the things on which we are prone to set our hearts and anchor our aspirations, the things for which we sweat and strive, ofttimes at the sacrifice of happiness and to the forfeiture of real success—these after all are but externals, the worth of which in the reckoning to come shall be counted in terms of the use we have made of them."[5]

Remember the story of the rich young man. He lived the commandments as he understood them, but when the Savior asked him to sell his possessions and give to the poor, the young man went away sorrowing because he could not relinquish his great wealth (see Matthew 19:16–22). Where our treasures are, there will our hearts be also (see Matthew 6:21). Consider your ways.

Consider your moral character. Before receiving my call as a General Authority, I was employed for twenty-one years by some of the great department stores in America. My life was blessed by close associations with some of the most talented leaders the retail industry ever produced. Nevertheless, when I compare those early associations with my current associations with the leadership of the Church, there is no comparison. The difference is not necessarily ability, but virtue. I have found that the brethren with whom I have associated in the Church over the last two decades represent the fulfillment of the promise given to the Prophet Joseph Smith: "Let virtue garnish thy thoughts unceasingly; then shall thy confidence wax strong in the presence of God; and the doctrine of the priesthood shall distil upon thy soul as the dews from heaven. The Holy Ghost shall be thy constant companion" (D&C 121:45–46).

I have watched my brethren, strengthened by the Holy Ghost as their constant companion, shoulder enormous workloads at an age when most men would be confined to rocking chairs. They are subjected to strenuous travel schedules but remain undeterred as they enthusiastically engage in building the kingdom of God. Recently, the realization came to me that the great spirit that attends my brethren, helping them magnify their assignments, is available to all the members of the Church. Everyone who earnestly seeks the Holy Ghost can be lifted and guided. As Elder James E. Talmage taught, "The special office of the Holy Ghost is to enlighten and ennoble the mind, to purify and sanctify the soul, to incite to good works, and to reveal the things of God."[6]

Consider your ways. Isn't the Holy Ghost a constant companion you need in your life?

Consider what you need to do to receive the full and rich blessings of the Spirit. Commence the inner cleansing—now!

I have always been grateful that I had the opportunity to serve for a time with President N. Eldon Tanner, who assumed much of the responsibility for the financial affairs of the Church. President Tanner was a man noted for his integrity and honesty. His immaculate moral character meant he could be trusted without question. Many times I sat next to President Tanner in meetings in which significant advantages were offered to the Church if it would only compromise on a little principle. President Tanner's voice would always speak passionately for what was right. He would never allow the Church to participate in anything that was not completely honest, legal, and ethical. President Tanner said, "There is far too much immorality, dishonesty, and lack of integrity in the lives of those who are leading and guiding the affairs of our nations, our schools, and our communities. Somehow we must get back to the lofty ideals . . . of those who fought and died for truth, religion, and freedom."[7]

Consider your ways.

Consider your religious practices. The words of James define pure religion. The brother of Christ wrote, "Pure religion and undefiled before God and the Father is this, To visit the fatherless and widows in their affliction, and to keep himself unspotted from the world" (James 1:27).

Consider your ways. Is religion an active, vital part of your life? Are you looking for or hiding from opportunities to serve? Are you anxiously engaged in good works?

Several years ago, I visited a high priests group meeting in a small community in southern Wyoming. The lesson that week was about losing one's life in service to others. As the lesson developed, it was evident that the teacher was well prepared to instruct his brethren. Then a comment by one of the brethren changed the whole tenor of the lesson. The brother said, "I have listened with great interest to the lesson today. The thought just crossed my mind that the information presented will soon be lost if we do not find applications for it."

This brother proposed a course of action. The night before, a good citizen of the community had passed away. His wife was a member of the Church, but he was not. The brother had visited the widow to offer his sympathies. As he left the home, his eyes wandered over their beautiful farm. The alfalfa was ready to cut, and the grain would soon be ready to harvest. He asked himself, "How will this poor sister cope with all her new responsibilities?" Certainly, she would need more time than her waiting crops would allow her. The course of action he proposed was for the high priests to help this widow operate her farm until a more permanent solution could be found. The balance of the group meeting was spent in organizing to assist her. The principle of the lesson had found immediate application.

Consider your ways. Do you pray daily? Do you study your scriptures consistently? Do you hold weekly family home evenings?

A home we purchased several years ago had a unique feature: a small study was equipped with a large closet, about one-fourth the size of the entire room. At first, we thought the closet was a design flaw, but it soon became one of my favorite places. There I could shut myself off from the cares of the world and earnestly communicate with my Heavenly Father. I took the opportunity to ask him what I needed to do to become more like him, and he took the opportunity to tell me. I found meaning in the Savior's instructions: "But thou, when thou prayest, enter into thy closet, and when thou hast shut thy door, pray to thy Father which is in secret; and thy Father which seeth in secret shall reward thee openly" (Matthew 6:6).

Consider your ways. Wouldn't your life be blessed by more open communication with your Heavenly Father? Couldn't you strive harder to learn his will for you and your family? If you were consistently to ask yourselves the question "What would the Savior do?" wouldn't it significantly change the way you look at life? Wouldn't it change your heart? Wouldn't you be born again?

Consider your ways. I know that Jesus Christ directs the affairs of this, his Church. If you have not yet received this same witness, isn't now the time to seek it? Consider your ways. Are they his ways?

NOTES

1. See Will Durant, *The Foundation of Civilization* (New York: Simon and Schuster, 1936), pp. 9–10; Will and Ariel Durant, *The Lessons of History* (New York: Simon and Schuster, 1968), pp. 87–94.

2. David O. McKay, *Gospel Ideals: Selections from the Discourses of David O. McKay* (Salt Lake City: Deseret News Press, 1953), p. 449.

3. Ibid., p. 490.

4. Conference Report, April 1938, p. 103.

5. *The Vitality of Mormonism* (Boston: Gorham Press, Richard G. Badger, 1919), p. 352.

6. James E. Talmage, *A Study of the Articles of Faith: Being a Consideration of the Principal Doctrines of The Church of Jesus Christ of Latter-day Saints* (Salt Lake City: Deseret Book Co., 1983), p. 167. Hereafter cited as *Articles of Faith*.

7. N. Eldon Tanner, "Remember Who You Are," *Ensign*, January 1983, pp. 3–4.

FRIENDSHIP

IN PROVERBS WE READ, "A friend loveth at all times" (Proverb 17:17). One of the great blessings of mortal life is good friends. President David O. McKay said:

> Among life's sweetest blessings is fellowship with men and women whose ideals and aspirations are high and noble. Next to a sense of a kinship with God comes the helpfulness, encouragement, and inspiration of friends. Friendship is a sacred possession. . . . One of the principal reasons which the Lord had for establishing His Church is to give all persons high and low, rich and poor, strong and feeble an opportunity to associate with their fellowmen in an atmosphere of uplifting, religious fellowship. This [association] may be found in Priesthood quorums, Auxiliaries, Sacrament meetings. He who neglects these opportunities, who fails to take advantage of them, to that extent starves his own soul.[1]

President McKay also said, "True friends enrich life. If you would have friends, be one."[2] The friends with whom we choose to associate are major contributors to the formation of our character. We form social habits by association with our friends. Good social habits can be useful and become the bases of wholesome personalities, but bad social habits can lead to antisocial attitudes and behaviors. Gradually, bad social habits tarnish our characters and severely limit our potential as sons and daughters of our Heavenly Father.

We can make friends by welcoming newcomers, deepening relationships with longtime acquaintances, and being more worthy friends to others. Friendships develop in different ways during different times in our lives, but each stage of life brings with it unique opportunities to make friends.

Our earliest friendships are often developed through family relationships. I was blessed to be a member of a loving family. I had three older sisters and two younger brothers as I was growing up. They were my best friends. We had a large backyard, a swing, a tree house, and a very large sandpile. All of these gave us places to play and enhance our family relationships. In times of stress, there was always the family to rely upon. At times of disappointment, the family offered comfort. In times of success, the family celebrated together.

Even today my brothers and sisters are my dearest and closest friends. I have the privilege of having two sisters living in the same condominium building where I live. One lives above me, and the other lives next door. One of our greatest joys is sitting on the balcony and watching the sunset while sharing fond memories of the past.

My school days offered significant opportunities to build friendships. Growing up in a Mormon community sometimes presented conflicts when choosing friends. School boundaries were usually much larger than ward boundaries, so on occasion I had to choose between school friends and Church friends. I was blessed to have both kinds of friends, but I usually found that Church friends were more reliable. They had the same ideals I was trying to maintain in my life. As I have attended some of my class reunions and renewed my acquaintance with my former schoolmates, I have found that friends who have maintained the Church standards have had richer, fuller, and happier lives than those without the light of the gospel in their lives.

The next friendships in my life were those with my missionary companions. We developed a real closeness from working together for a common purpose and being on our knees together so many times during the day. There is something special about friendships that develop from engaging in service. Do you remember the example of the Savior as he met with the apostles at the

Last Supper? He wanted to serve them, so he girded himself with a towel and went to each of them and washed their feet. Then after washing their feet, he said, "Ye call me Master and Lord: and ye say well; for so I am. If I then, your Lord and Master, have washed your feet; ye also ought to wash one another's feet. For I have given you an example, that ye should do as I have done to you" (John 13:13–15).

After my mission came service in the U.S. Marine Corps. During the weeks I was in basic training, some of the marines in my unit encouraged me to go on weekend leaves with them. I resisted because I knew how they acted and what kind of language they used around the camp. Finally, after a few weeks, they persuaded me one Saturday evening to go into Los Angeles with them. We rode the bus into the city and then planned to take a streetcar to a dance hall.

As we boarded the streetcar, my companions began to flirt with girls that I found unattractive because of the way they dressed and acted. I knew right then that I had made a major mistake. I started to move away toward the rear of the car. I sat down next to a group of young people who looked more wholesome. I asked where they were going, and they said, "To a dance." "Where?" I asked. They said, "You probably don't know much about this place. It's the Adams Ward of the LDS Church. Would you like to join us?" Were they surprised when I told them I was a member of the Church. I got off the streetcar with them at the Adams Ward and shared a delightful time with the new friends I made that evening—friends who shared the same values that I did.

My next set of friendships I made in college. Here again I was presented with a choice—I could either join a fraternity or participate in activities at the Latter-day Saint institute. After carefully considering both, I selected the institute. It was through the LDS institute in Logan, Utah, that I met Virginia Lee, who would become my wife. There is not a friend as close and loving, as caring, and as fun to be with as the one the Lord gives to you as an eternal companion. The right friendships in college helped me establish an eternal friendship and form an eternal companion-ship.

Professional life is another area that provides opportunities for friendships. When I was working in Sacramento, California, I was offered an exciting job in New York City. My current employers tried to talk me into staying in California and used the argument that I would be unhappy on the East Coast. They said I would not like the unfriendliness of easterners. They told me that people there would push and shove and try to walk all over you if you allowed them to do it. It was every man for himself without any thought for his neighbors.

Being a small-town Utah boy, I couldn't believe that people could live the way they described. It made me want to go to New York City all the more just to prove they were wrong.

After only six months of working in New York, however, I was ready to concede that my California friends were right. But then I realized that I hadn't made much of an effort at extending myself. I started on a planned and systematic effort to determine whether the people in New York City really deserved their reputation.

My first thought was to start with the commuters with whom I rode into the city each day. I lived in Scarsdale, which was about a forty-five-minute train ride from downtown New York. Because the train always ran exactly on schedule, I realized my behavior followed a rather predictable pattern. I started noticing the habits of the other commuters. They would leave home at exactly the same minute each morning, walk to the station, buy a *New York Times,* walk down to a certain board on the platform, fold their newspapers a certain way, stand on that board until the train arrived, get on the same car each morning, try to find the same seat on the train, and read their newspapers the same way all the way into Grand Central Station. They would never speak to one another or show any signs of friendliness.

I decided that the only way to get to know anybody was to break his routine. I selected a man with whom I thought I would like to get acquainted, and after observing his routine for a few days, I initiated a counter-routine. I arrived at the train station at about the same time he did, watched him put his dime on the tray to purchase a newspaper, and as soon as he started to walk down to his favorite board on the platform, I broke into a run, just beating him there, and firmly planted myself. You should have seen the look on his face. He came up to me and stood just as close to his spot as he could without stepping on my toes. As the crowd gathered and started to push and shove, he tried to move me away from the position I had established. Fortunately, I was pretty good sized and didn't budge an inch. This unnerved him so that he didn't even take time to unfold his newspaper. I just didn't take any notice of him, firmly holding my ground.

When the train arrived, I quickly jumped on and took his favorite seat. He was forced to sit in the middle of a three-seater just in front of me. He rode all the way into the city visibly disturbed. I could see the red, flushed condition on the back of his neck. I believe I ruined the entire day for him. The next morning I repeated the same process. His neck was scarlet this time; it brightened up the whole car.

The most remarkable thing happened the third morning. When I arrived at the train platform, he was already there with two feet firmly planted on his favorite board, reading his newspaper. I couldn't help but laugh out loud when I saw him. He gave me a scowl, and then he couldn't hold back either. I introduced myself as a new arrival from California, determined to break up the routine of a New York commuter. We had an enjoyable visit on the train platform that morning. We got on the train and sat together all the way into New York and had a delightful ride.

From then on, breaking up each other's routine became a game. Each morning we would race down the platform trying to beat the other one to that favorite spot. Soon others on the platform started to notice what we were doing, and before you knew it, there were three, then four, then five, then ten, all racing for that particular board each morning. It almost got out of hand, as we noticed some men in the back exchanging dollar bills with another man. We asked what was going on, and they said they were betting who would be on the board first the following morning.

The great friendships I made with my fellow commuters endured for many, many years. The so-called cold New Yorker was just as friendly and warm as anyone else. All I had to do was break through a thick, inner-city shell to enjoy warm, close friendships.

I have found that the right friends have a powerful influence on our lives. Choose your friends wisely! Make certain they will complement your life goals and help to build within you the right values and standards. How do we develop better friendships? A Church tract printed many years ago gives us several ideas. It lists the following helps:

1. Be sincere.

2. Become thoroughly acquainted by learning their names and other important things about them, being a good listener, and discussing their interests. Show interest in them, their hobbies, their work, their children.

3. Be unselfish.

4. Show brotherly love and concern for them. Meet their needs by giving them helpful service.

5. Graciously let them be of service to you when they offer.

6. Smile and be positive.

The Book of Mormon tells us about Alma and his friends, the sons of Mosiah, and the joy that came to them when they met after many years of separation. As you remember, Alma and the sons of Mosiah were quite the rascals in their younger years; and then through a marvelous visitation, their lives changed. From then on, they lived lives of service to others. Alma served the Church, and the sons of Mosiah went on missions to carry the good news of the gospel to their Lamanite brothers and sisters.

In the book of Alma, chapter 17, we read of their reunion after many years of separation:

> And now it came to pass that as Alma was journeying from the land of Gideon southward, away to the land of Manti, behold, to his astonishment, he met with the sons of Mosiah journeying towards the land of Zarahemla.
>
> Now these sons of Mosiah were with Alma at the time the angel first appeared unto him; therefore Alma did rejoice

exceedingly to see his brethren; and what added more to his joy, they were still his brethren in the Lord; yea, and they had waxed strong in the knowledge of the truth; for they were men of a sound understanding and they had searched the scriptures diligently, that they might know the word of God.

But this is not all; they had given themselves to much prayer, and fasting; therefore they had the spirit of prophecy, and the spirit of revelation, and when they taught, they taught with power and authority of God. (Alma 17:1–3)

Do you see what had happened? They remained true and faithful to their friendship by living up to the standards they had set for each other. Because they were still brethren in the Lord, the joy of their reunion was great.

True friends do indeed enrich one's life, as President McKay stated. I thank the Lord for the friends who have blessed my life. I urge you to make an effort to cultivate friendships with those around you who can become your brethren and sisters in the Lord.

Notes

1. Conference Report, April 1940, p. 116.

2. As quoted in Conference Report, April 1963, p. 32.

BEING IN THE WORLD

From the teachings of the Savior, the members of the Church have adopted a common expression: we talk of being *in* the world but not *of* the world (see John 17:14–16). Normally, we say this to emphasize our need to remain free from the sin and materialism so prevalent in the world in which we live. The importance of not being of the world cannot be overstated. We should continually remind ourselves to keep our lives in harmony with the Lord's teachings. However, I choose to discuss the first part of the expression: being in the world.

It is in the world where we have been privileged to come and enjoy a mortal experience. It is in the world that we are to be tested and tried. It is in the world where we have opportunities to participate in sacred, saving ordinances that will determine our postmortal life. It is in the world where we have an opportunity to serve and make our contributions to mankind. It is to this world the Savior must come.

Our prophets have encouraged us to be mindful of our obligations while we are here in the world. President David O. McKay said:

> The responsibility of showing to the world that the gospel of Jesus Christ will solve its problems rests upon the men who make the claim. . . . I believe . . . that every *world problem may be solved by obedience to the principles of the gospel of Jesus Christ.* . . .
>
> The solution of the great world problems is here in the Church of Jesus Christ. Ample provision is made not only for the

needs of individuals, but also for nation and groups of nations. I realize that it is a great claim. . . . It is simply the application of God's plan to the world problems. You who hold the priesthood have greater responsibility today, now that you live in this creative moment in the world's history, than ever the Church has had before. I repeat it. If we make the claim to hold the truth, it is obligatory upon every Latter-day Saint so to live, that when the people of the world come, in answer to the call, to test the fruit of the tree, they will find it wholesome and good.

The Lord help us to be able to prove to the world that we possess just what the world today is longing for, and when they see it, may they know, as you know, as I know, that the everlasting gospel is a light to the world.[1]

In the Old Testament, I found a classic example of someone who lived *in* the world but not *of* the world, influencing it through his righteous living. The birth of this young man came at a time when Israel was a conquered nation. The Israelites were doomed to lives of servitude, yet this man rose above his adverse circumstances to rule over those who had been his conquerors.

After the death of King Solomon in 975 B.C., the ten tribes revolted and separated themselves from the tribe of Judah. A divided Israel was not able to defend itself against the other powers in the region. Egypt and Assyria took turns conquering the lands of Israel. In the year 607 B.C., Assyria proper and the northern provinces fell into the hands of the Medes, while Syria lay open to be seized by the Babylonians.

In the midst of this struggle, it seemed an appropriate time for Egypt to attack Palestine. The king of the Babylonians sent his son, Nebuchadnezzar, to drive the Egyptians back. While the battle raged against the Egyptians, the king passed away and Nebuchadnezzar became the ruler of Babylonia. He was successful against the Egyptians and became ruler over all of Syria to the Egyptian border. He ruled by terror, crushing his enemies by fire and sword and weakening them with wholesale deportations to other parts of his empire.

This was the time during which Daniel was born. As a youth, he and certain other Hebrews were taken to be trained for service in the court of Nebuchadnezzar. They were chosen because of their wisdom and knowledge and ability to learn. Thus, Daniel was brought into a strange land with strange customs, a strange environment, and a very different religious heritage.

Daniel's first test in being "in the world" came when the servant of Nebuchadnezzar ordered him to drink of his wines and eat of the "king's meat." Daniel "purposed in his heart that he would not defile himself with the portion of the king's meat, nor with the wine which he drank" (Daniel 1:8).

The servant argued that the king had made him responsible for the training of these young men and had commanded that they should eat and drink the same as the others. If they did not, the king would see that they were growing weak and thin and would surely have his servant killed. Then Daniel begged that he and his friends be allowed to follow the health habits their people had received through revelation. He requested a test: for ten days they would feed upon grains and drink water, then see if they were as healthy as the rest.

Daniel's strategy was most interesting. He did not challenge the beliefs of the Babylonians. Instead, he volunteered to participate in a test to determine which way was the best. The servant agreed to the test, and for the next ten days, Daniel and those who were with him ate and drank only the things they knew they should. At the end of ten days, Daniel and his friends were found to be healthier and stronger than all the rest. Daniel's beliefs were verified. He did not need to adopt different standards of the world even though he was in the world.

As a young executive many years ago, part of my job involved attending dinners sponsored by different business groups. Each dinner was preceded by a social hour. I felt uncomfortable in these settings. After the first one or two dinners, I started coming late to miss the social hour. My boss thought this was not a good practice, because I would be missing some valued time associating with business leaders. Still, I felt awkward visiting in groups where I was the only one without a drink in my hand. I kept wondering what to do with my hands. You can always put one hand in your pocket, but you look foolish with both of them there. I tried holding a glass of 7-Up, but it had the same appearance as an alcoholic beverage.

I finally went over to the bartender and asked if he had any drink that was distinctively different in appearance from an alcoholic beverage. He went into the kitchen and came back with a half gallon of milk and poured me a glass. Drinking a glass of milk at a cocktail hour was a unique practice. It seemed to attract everyone's attention, and I became the target of a lot of jesting. It embarrassed me at first, until I discovered that I was meeting more business leaders than I had at any previous gathering. I found that I did not have to violate Church standards to become a viable, contributing member in my chosen profession. It was more the case that success came because I *did* adhere to my values.

As the word spread, it soon became a standard practice to have a carton of milk at the bar. I was amazed, as time passed, by how many of my associates were joining me for a glass of milk during the social hour. I found, just as Daniel did, that although being different in the world brought some interesting reactions, obedience to the Lord's law is always associated with his blessings.

Isn't this the same message as the revelation contained in the Doctrine and Covenants? It reads, "There is a law, irrevocably decreed in heaven before the foundations of this world, upon which all blessings are predicated—and when we obtain any blessing from God, it is by obedience to that law upon which it is predicated" (D&C 130:20–21).

In addition to being obedient to the word of the Lord, we have been instructed in our responsibilities to declare the gospel to *all* of our Father in Heaven's children. In the Doctrine and Covenants we read:

> Remember the worth of souls is great in the sight of God. . . .
> And how great is his joy in the soul that repenteth!
> Wherefore, you are called to cry repentance unto this people.
> And if it so be that you should labor all your days in crying repentance unto this people, and bring, save it be one soul unto me, how great shall be your joy with him in the kingdom of my Father!

And now, if your joy will be great with one soul that you
have brought unto me into the kingdom of my Father, how
great will be your joy if you should bring many souls unto me!
(D&C 18:10, 13–16)

I don't know how we can experience this joy if we are not willing to reach out beyond our own circle of church friends. We live
in the world during our mortal experience. The Christian principles the gospel teaches are needed in all we do and among all
peoples.

The influence we radiate as we uphold righteous principles
can make worthwhile contributions in the world. A righteous
example can attract others to living standards established by the
Lord for the conduct of his children here in mortality. A righteous
example can bring souls to the light of the gospel, encouraging
some to join the Church. Embracing the gospel is a personal decision, and we always respect and understand the agency of individuals, but how can we expect our brothers and sisters in the world
to embrace righteous principles if we do not extend our influence
outward to make them aware of those principles?

Our governments need standards of integrity. Our communities need yardsticks for measuring decency. Our neighborhoods
need models of beauty and cleanliness. Our schools need continued encouragement and assistance in maintaining high educa-
tional standards. Rather than spend time complaining about the
direction in which these institutions are going, we need to exert
our influence to point them in the right direction. A small effort
by a few can result in so much good for so many.

Sometimes I think we fear participation because of the oppo-
sition we may face. In the example of Daniel, we also see a later
instance in which he met head-on the challenge of being in the
world and in which he was able to influence those around him for
good. As Daniel's talents were recognized by the king, he became a
trusted counselor. Many were jealous of the position this outsider
had gained, and they sought to do away with him. They devised a
new law that would prevent Daniel from praying to God, the
Eternal Father. The penalty for breaking the law was to be cast into

the lions' den. Daniel was discovered praying, and the penalty was executed. But because of Daniel's faith in God, the lions did not harm him.

Daniel was able to rise above the many challenges presented him by his enemies and still live his religion. The Lord blessed and protected him in his righteousness.

Not only did Daniel's service benefit the king; the faith Daniel had in the Lord affected an entire kingdom. The king sent forth a decree "that in every dominion of [the] kingdom men tremble and fear before the God of Daniel: for he is the living God" (Daniel 6:26). Great was the service of one righteous man, serving in the world of his captors. Great will be the results as *we* serve, each in our own personal way, in the world in which *we* live.

May we have the necessary faith to place our trust in the Lord. May we not worry about the forces that will surely oppose righteousness. May we have the courage to move forward in the cause of truth.

As we live in the world, may we contribute by making it a better place through our righteous living, our service in causes that are just, and our faith that good will always triumph over evil.

NOTE

1. *Gospel Ideals* (Salt Lake City: Improvement Era, 1953), p. 5.

10

STAND FIRM IN YOUR CONVICTIONS

BRIGHAM YOUNG once counseled us to use the scriptures as follows: "Do you read the Scriptures, my brethren and sisters, as though you were writing them a thousand, two thousand, or five thousand years ago? Do you read them as though you stood in the place of the men who wrote them? If you do not feel thus, it is your privilege to do so, that you may be as familiar with the spirit and meaning of the written word of God as you are with your daily walk and conversation."[1]

The Book of Mormon has many special accounts with lessons that can be applied to all ages of time. It is a book of great passion and feeling. Let us take Brigham Young's advice and imagine we are standing in the place where Moroni, the last of the great Nephite prophets, stood. The assignment his father gave him to complete the record entrusted to his care was very difficult.

He must have mourned as he described how his people had been hunted by the Lamanites until they were all destroyed. Imagine the loneliness he experienced as he reported that his father was among those who were killed. We sense that after that great destruction, the only thing Moroni was living for was to complete the record. He wrote, "Therefore I will write and hide up the records in the earth; and whither I go it mattereth not" (Mormon 8:4).

All that sustained Moroni is the faith that the Lord would preserve him long enough to complete the record and the knowledge that someday that record would be found by one chosen of the

Lord. He realized that the record would be a voice of warning to nations of the consequences of turning away from the teachings of the Lord.

It is from the depths of his heart that Moroni cries out to those who will eventually receive this record. He wants to spare those who read his account the heartache and misery that come from disobedience to God's laws.

Moroni writes, first, to the members of the Church, and then to those who have not embraced the gospel of Jesus Christ. His last words to the members of the Church are words of warning. He writes as one who sees the social forces that destroyed his people repeating themselves in the future:

> Behold, the Lord hath shown unto me great and marvelous things concerning that which must shortly come, at that day when these things shall come forth among you.
>
> Behold, I speak unto you as if ye were present, and yet ye are not. But behold, Jesus Christ hath shown you unto me, and I know your doing.
>
> And I know that ye do walk in the pride of your hearts; and there are none save a few only who do not lift themselves up in the pride of their hearts, unto the wearing of very fine apparel, unto envying, and strifes, and malice, and persecutions, and all manner of iniquities; and your churches, yea, even every one, have become polluted because of the pride of your hearts.
>
> For behold, ye do love money, and your substance, and your fine apparel, and the adorning of your churches, more than ye love the poor and the needy, the sick and the afflicted.
>
> O ye pollutions, ye hypocrites, ye teachers, who sell yourselves for that which will canker, why have ye polluted the holy church of God? Why are ye ashamed to take upon you the name of Christ? Why do ye not think that greater is the value of an endless happiness than that misery which never dies—because of the praise of the world? (Mormon 8:34–38)

I guess one of the greatest mysteries of human history is why people fail to learn from the past. In the case of the Church, why do those who profess to be true followers of Christ repeatedly become victims of the enticements of the world? The evidence is strong regarding the blessings that accrue to those who trust in and follow the ways prescribed by the Lord, yet so many members of the Church fail to heed the evidence.

Many of us are more concerned about our fine apparel, the size of our houses, and our luxury cars than we are about assisting the poor and the needy. The forces promoting legalized abortion, gambling, pornography, and banning of public prayer also threaten the values that bind us together as a community of Saints.

Clearly, the members of the Church face tremendous challenges in the latter days. We must not only resist but mount a counteroffensive against the temptations and teachings of the world if we are to remain a distinctive people.

Despite the challenges we face, I plead with each of you to stand firm in your convictions. There is no escape from the whirlwind of judgments God will unleash on the heads of his children who choose to pursue a course that is against his will. We need to heed Moroni's warning to avoid the fate that destroyed his people.

Part of what Moroni was feeling should also be translated into a renewed desire to do missionary service. Moroni witnessed the wickedness and destruction that come from unbelief, when men's and women's souls are not anchored to the teachings of the gospel. After warning the believers, he pleads with the unbelievers:

> And now, I speak also concerning those who do not believe in Christ.
>
> Behold, will ye believe in the day of your visitation—behold, when the Lord shall come, yea, even that great day when the earth shall be rolled together as a scroll, and the elements shall melt with fervent heat, yea, in that great day when ye shall be brought to stand before the Lamb of God—then will ye say that there is no God?
>
> Then will ye longer deny the Christ, or can ye behold the Lamb of God? Do ye suppose that ye shall dwell with him under a consciousness of your guilt? Do ye suppose that ye could be happy to dwell with that holy Being, when your souls are racked with a consciousness of guilt that ye have ever abused his laws? . . .
>
> O then ye unbelieving, turn ye unto the Lord; cry mightily unto the Father in the name of Jesus, that perhaps ye may be found spotless, pure, fair, and white, having been cleansed by

the blood of the Lamb, at that great and last day. (Mormon 9:1–3, 6)

Who can ignore a voice of warning from one who witnessed so much heartache and misery? Is it any wonder that his words declare that there is a better, happier, more fulfilling way to live? Moroni's words are not just a voice of warning but also a voice of hope. He reminds us that every one of God's children are precious to Him. Our Heavenly Father desires that every soul enjoy immortality and eternal life.

Continuing with Moroni's counsel, we read:

> Because of the redemption of man, which came by Jesus Christ, they are brought back into the presence of the Lord; yea, this is wherein all men are redeemed, because the death of Christ bringeth to pass the resurrection, which bringeth to pass a redemption from an endless sleep, from which sleep all men shall be awakened by the power of God when the trump shall sound; and they shall come forth, both small and great, and all shall stand before his bar, being redeemed and loosed from this eternal band of death, which death is a temporal death.
>
> And then cometh the judgment of the Holy One upon them; and then cometh the time that he that is filthy shall be filthy still; and he that is righteous shall be righteous still; he that is happy shall be happy still; and he that is unhappy shall be unhappy still. (Mormon 9:13–14)

The restored gospel of our Lord and Savior is available to bless all the children of our Father in Heaven. Members of the Church should be anxious to share the gospel and all its saving principles. President Spencer W. Kimball declared, "Our objective is to bring the gospel to all the world. . . . This is an ambitious project we have, but as you know, we are but planning to do what the Lord has already seen and [that] which he has charged us with."[2]

Today we find ourselves surrounded by so much depression, despair, lack of confidence, and loss of hope. I ask myself: for what purpose is all this gloom? Consider with me for a moment the great blessings we have been promised in a covenant with the Lord. He has entered into a binding and solemn contract with each of us to give us all that he has, according to our faithfulness.

He has declared, "I, the Lord, am bound when ye do what I say" (D&C 82:10).

By solemn covenant, the Lord will fulfill his part of the agreement. The opportunity to receive these great blessings is based on our individual worthiness. What is required of us?

First, we need to be obedient to the laws of the Lord. This is one of the first lessons taught to Adam and Eve: Obedience brings faith. It brings forth the blessings of heaven. Disobedience brings forth heartache and despair.

Following the law of obedience comes the requirement to give of ourselves in service to our Heavenly Father's children. Sacrificing what we have to benefit our brothers and sisters is the crowning test of the gospel. One of the purposes of this mortal experience is to see if we will follow the Savior's counsel to "seek ye first the kingdom of God, and his righteousness" (Matthew 6:33).

We live in the most glorious era in the history of mankind. The opportunity to reap the blessings of the Lord is greater than ever before, as is the opportunity to serve him and experience the the eternal satisfaction that accompanies that service.

Let the words of Moroni and the voices of all the prophets fill our hearts and our souls. Let us learn from history that "wickedness never was happiness" (Alma 41:10). Let us remember that it is in our power to enjoy the fruits the Lord has promised us—if we meet the requirements of being obedient to his law and rendering unto him what he requires of us in service and sacrifice.

NOTES

1. *Discourses of Brigham Young,* sel. John A. Widtsoe (Salt Lake City: Deseret Book Co., 1954), p. 128.

2. Address given at regional representatives' seminar, Salt Lake City, 5 April 1976, p. 1.

STAYING POWER

JOHN WOODEN, the legendary UCLA basketball coach, was a man who understood what it takes to succeed. In his forty years of coaching, he worked at UCLA for twenty-seven years, during which his teams never had a losing season. In fact, he led his teams to ten national championships in his last twelve years at UCLA.

Coach Wooden cited some of the reasons for his "staying power": "I emphasized constant improvement and steady performance. I have often said, 'The mark of a true champion is to always perform near your own level of competency.'"

The well-known coach commented that he probably scouted opponents less than any other coach he knew—less, in fact, than most high school coaches. Instead he taught his players the basics, because he recognized that sound offensive and defensive principles would serve them well no matter what style of play they encountered.

He was as concerned with a player's character as he was with the player's ability. "While it may be possible to reach the top of one's profession on sheer ability," he said, "it is impossible to stay there without hard work and character." Wooden looked for athletes who played a clean game and who were constantly trying to improve themselves in order to strengthen the team. "Then, if their ability warranted it," he explained, "the championships would take care of themselves."[1]

Coach Wooden identified some important principles that were the bedrock of his championship teams. Perhaps we can apply those same principles as we work to better ourselves as a community of Saints. First, consistently do your best with the talents your Father in Heaven has given you. Second, concentrate on the basics, because they are appropriate in any situation or season of life. Third, worry more about developing sound character than about building reputation.

Consistently do your best. One of my favorite scriptures is found in the eighth chapter of Psalms:

> O Lord our Lord, how excellent is thy name in all the earth! who hast set thy glory above the heavens. . . .
>
> When I consider thy heavens, and the work of thy fingers, the moon and the stars, which thou hast ordained;
>
> What is man, that thou art mindful of him? and the son of man, that thou visitest him?
>
> For thou hast made him a little lower than the angels, and hast crowned him with glory and honour. (Psalm 8:1, 3–5)

I like to think of myself as a junior angel with the power and potential of an eternal being.

I am absolutely amazed as I watch the growth and development of my grandchildren. I marvel at how different they are in appearance and personality, even though they come from a common heritage and similar environments.

Let me describe the oldest sons of my three children. The son of my eldest daughter is a serious student. He ranks number one in his class; he is very disciplined; he schedules himself very carefully. When I baby-sit at his house, this is a common source of frustration. The children gather around me for a story before they retire to bed. I am just getting to the good part of the story when the clock strikes the hour. My grandson then announces to his brother and sister that it is time to go to bed. He does not allow me to finish the page, not even a sentence. The established bedtime has arrived—end of story.

My son's eldest boy is a great debater. He has a sound argument, supported by numerous facts, against everything he doesn't want to do. His reasoning is often brilliant. He also has an attention span that is most uncommon for a child his age. He is unusually fascinated by animal and insect life. Once I watched him sit for hours watching a spider consuming a fly entrapped in its web.

The son of my youngest daughter is fascinated by anything mechanical. When he had just learned to walk, I took him on a tour of Temple Square to show him the beautiful flowers, trees, and buildings. He had no interest in them. He spent his time finding all the sprinkler heads on the grounds, testing them to see if they were screwed in tightly.

Three boys springing from the same family tree—how different each of them is in appearance and talent!

All of us are endowed with abundant talent, beauty, and ability. Our lack of productivity can never be blamed on a lack of raw material. Richard L. Evans once wrote:

> We know of no one in life who isn't an Important Person. We know of no man on the street (or in the gutter, for that matter) who isn't a child of God with the same rights and with the same relationship to his Father in heaven as all the rest of us have.
>
> We know of no one, young or old, from infants to elderly individuals, whose past or whose potential we would want to appraise as being unimportant. We know of no one we might see in any public place—on subways or buses, or walking in shabby shoes—or any boy selling papers . . . who doesn't have an inestimable, unknown potential, here and hereafter.[2]

I was thrilled with the talk Peter Vidmar gave in the priesthood session of general conference after he had successfully won his gold medals in the Olympics. His theme was that the Lord had blessed him with a talent. It was his responsibility to make himself a champion. Brother Vidmar's formula was simple. He spent fifteen minutes longer each day perfecting his routines than anyone who competed against him. The multiplication of those extra fifteen minutes daily gave him the edge and prepared him for his goal of becoming an Olympic champion. He consistently did his best with his God-given talents, and he was blessed with the success he sought.

Concentrate on the basics. Coach Wooden taught basic principles to his players, guidelines like "Never give the outside to any forward who tries to drive around you." The game of life is also governed by some basic principles. Two of the more important principles we live by are integrity and honesty.

The Lord loves those who have integrity. He said about the Prophet's brother, Hyrum Smith, "Blessed is my servant Hyrum Smith; for I, the Lord, love him because of the integrity of his heart, and because he loveth that which is right before me, saith the Lord" (D&C 124:15).

What is the meaning of integrity? We can find several definitions in the dictionary: rigid adherence to a code or standard of values; moral soundness, especially as it relates to steadfastness to truth, purpose, responsibility, or trust; moral and ethical strength; or the quality of being whole, complete, undivided.

The Lord described Job as a man who was perfect and upright. As Job was suffering untold trials and tribulations, his wife said to him, "Does thou still retain thine integrity?" (Job 2:9). Even with all his problems and challenges, Job "sinned not" (Job 1:22). And the Lord said, "There is none like him in the earth, a perfect and an upright man, one that feareth God, and escheweth evil . . . and still he holdeth fast his integrity" (Job 2:3).

When Job's friends falsely accused him of sin, he said:

> All the while my breath is in me, and the spirit of God is in my nostrils;
> My lips shall not speak wickedness, nor my tongue utter deceit.
> God forbid that I should justify you: till I die I will not remove mine integrity from me.
> My righteousness I hold fast, and will not let it go. (Job 27:3–6)

Job invited judgment from God so "that God may know mine integrity" (Job 31:6). Job's conscience was clear, for he knew he was honest and upright in all of his endeavors, and he would never compromise his integrity.

Many years ago when the railroad was just beginning to cross the country regularly, President Brigham Young said to a group of Church members:

We want the Saints to increase in goodness, until our mechanics, for instance, are so honest and reliable that this Railroad Company will say, 'Give us a Mormon elder for an engineer, then none need have the least fear to ride, for if he knows there is danger he will take every measure necessary to preserve the lives of those entrusted to his care.' I want to see our elders so full of integrity that they will be preferred by this Company for their engine builders, watchmen, engineers, clerks and business managers.[3]

Abraham Lincoln said, "I am not bound to win, but I am bound to be true. I am not bound to succeed, but I am bound to live up to what light I have."[4] Lincoln is remembered for what he did but also for what he was—a forthright man of integrity.

The principle of honesty is a close relation to that of integrity. Our thirteenth article of faith begins with the statement "We believe in being honest." We do not believe in honesty merely as a matter of policy. Honesty is a principle of salvation in the kingdom of God.

Moses gave us the following counsel: "If a man vow a vow unto the Lord, or swear an oath to bind his soul with a bond; he shall not break his word, he shall do according to all that proceedeth out of his mouth" (Numbers 30:2).

I learned early in my business career that dishonesty is like a disease. It requires a strong antidote to effect a cure. It seemed that every time I was compassionate and gave a dishonest person a second chance, I lived to regret it. It seemed that once they lost their honesty, they had to hit bottom and suffer severe consequences before there was any hope for a permanent cure.

It was Brigham Young who said, "Simple truth, simplicity, honesty uprightness, justice, mercy, love, kindness, do good to all and evil to none, how easy it is to live by such principles! A thousand times easier than to practice deception!"[5]

Develop sound character. President David O. McKay related the experience of standing in a sculptor's yard in Florence, Italy. There he observed broken, irregular pieces of granite from which the sculptor created works of art. In the yard he also observed a magnificent figure, a statue of David, carved more than four hundred years ago from pieces of stone as crude as those around the yard. He compared the carving of stone to the carving of a soul and asked the question "Is it going to be a deformed one, or is it going to be something admired and beautiful for time and throughout eternity?"

President McKay's account reminds us that it is our responsibility to carve out our own lives, to carve out the character we would like to have. Our tools are our ideas and thoughts.

Charles Reade said, "Sow an act, and you reap a habit. Sow a habit, and you reap a character. Sow a character, and you reap a destiny."[6]

We become what we think and do. Habits mold our character. Good habits are not acquired from good intentions only; they are developed in the workshop of our daily lives. They are fashioned in the often uneventful, commonplace routines of life and strengthened by practice.

Brigham Young University president Ernest L. Wilkinson once said, "Good character is not something to be obtained by ease and indulgence, or by something socially agreeable. It cannot be acquired by absorption or by proxy, or on the auction block. It is a reward derived from honest trial in overcoming difficulties. We grow by mastering tasks which others consider to be impossible."

This very day you are forming habits that will be part of your life forever. Samuel Johnson, one of England's famous authors, wrote, "The chains of habits are generally too small to be felt until they are too strong to be broken."[7]

Positive habits are as difficult to make as negative habits are difficult to break. It takes desire, repetition, and time to form them.

The prophets through the ages have counseled and encouraged each of us to develop a sound character. Paul's warning to the Galatians applies to all of us:

> Be not deceived; God is not mocked: for whatsoever a man soweth, that shall he also reap.
> For he that soweth to his flesh shall of the flesh reap corrup-

tion; but he that soweth to the Spirit shall of the Spirit reap life everlasting.

And let us not be weary in well doing: for in due season we shall reap, if we faint not. (Galatians 6:7–9)

If we sow seeds of decency and goodness, the fruits of our honest labors will be blessings in heaven.

Hold fast to those basic principles that are tried and true. Consistently develop your talents, protect and preserve your honesty and integrity, and build a sound character. This is the secret of real staying power, for these are principles that will not depreciate with time. Why? Because they are God-given principles founded on eternal truths.

NOTES

1. *Wall Street Journal,* 23 April 1986, p. 39.

2. Richard L. Evans, Jr., *Richard L. Evans—The Man and the Message* (Salt Lake City: Bookcraft, 1973), p. 304.

3. Brigham Young, in *Journal of Discourses,* 12:300.

4. *Vital Quotations,* comp. Emerson Roy West (Salt Lake City: Bookcraft, 1968), p.178.

5. *Discourses of Brigham Young,* sel. John A. Widtsoe (Salt Lake City: Deseret Book Co., 1954), p. 232.

6. *The Oxford University Press Dictionary of Quotations,* 2d ed. (London: Chancellor Press, 1985), p. 406.

7. *The International Dictionary of Thoughts,* comp. John P. Bradley et al. (Chicago: J. G. Ferguson Publishing Co., 1969), p. 348.

MEANINGFUL CELEBRATIONS

EVERY YEAR, all peoples and all nations celebrate special events in their histories. Christians throughout the world observe Christmas and Easter to celebrate, but more especially to remember the birth and glorious resurrection of Jesus Christ. In the United States, celebrations are also held on Independence Day, July 4, commemorating the declaration of political sovereignty of this great nation. All members of the Church, but especially those residing in Utah, celebrate July 24, or Pioneer Day, the day the Mormon pioneers arrived in the Salt Lake Valley.

Meaningful celebrations focus our thoughts on history. They afford us an opportunity to review the past. We glean perspective and wisdom from the experiences of the past as we anticipate the future. Cicero wrote this of history: "Not to know what has been transacted in former times is to be always a child. If no use is made of the labors of past ages, the world must remain always in the infancy of knowledge."[1]

Recent events have rekindled in me an interest in our church heritage and history. I have become especially fascinated by the similarities between the Hebrew nation and our own church history.

The man prepared by Heavenly Father to free and lead the nation of Israel was Moses. The Lord revealed through Moses the feasts and events the Israelites should hold as perpetual reminders of their deliverance from slavery and the birth of their new nation. These celebrations took two forms. First were the celebrations of actual historical events, such as the Passover, to remind the people of the Lord's hand in delivering them. In addition, there were traditions tied to periods of time determined by various multiples of the number seven.

Of course, the seventh day was the Sabbath, a day of rest. The seventh month was a time of harvest. Then, as we read in chapter 25 of Leviticus, there were special instructions pertaining to the seventh year *and* the fiftieth year:

> Six years thou shalt sow thy field, and six years thou shalt prune thy vineyard, and gather in the fruit thereof;
>
> But in the seventh year shall be a sabbath of rest unto the land, a sabbath for the Lord: thou shalt neither sow thy field, nor prune thy vineyard....
>
> And thou shalt number seven sabbaths of years unto thee, seven times seven years; and the space of the seven sabbaths of years shall be unto thee forty and nine years.
>
> Then shalt thou cause the trumpet of the jubile to sound on the tenth day of the seventh month, in the day of atonement shall ye make the trumpet sound throughout all your land.
>
> And ye shall hallow the fiftieth year, and proclaim liberty throughout all the land unto all the inhabitants thereof: it shall be a jubile unto you; and ye shall return every man unto his possession, and ye shall return every man unto his family. (Leviticus 25:3–4, 8–10)

Every fiftieth year, the land was to be returned to the original owners or their descendants; all Israelites sold into slavery for debt were to be freed; and the land, as in the seventh or sabbatical year, was to lie fallow.

Even in our day, the tradition of the sabbatical year is perpetuated by universities that encourage faculty members to go on sabbaticals, roughly every seventh year. The word *jubilee* is derived from a Hebrew word meaning "ram's horn," no doubt referring to the horn used to proclaim the beginning of the jubilee year, or the fiftieth year.

Four purposes for the celebrations and traditions of ancient Israel could be applied to celebrations in our day to guide and influence the way we celebrate and the meaning we give to our celebrations.

First, meaningful celebrations preserved the religious faith and strengthened the spiritual fiber of the people of Israel. This is clear from the messages associated with the celebration of the jubilee year. An excerpt from *The International Standard Bible Encyclopedia* states:

> The fiftieth year was to be a time of proclaiming liberty to all the inhabitants of the land. God had redeemed His people from bondage in Egypt; and none of them was again to be reduced to the status of . . . slave. . . . God's chosen child was not to be oppressed. . . . Indeed, as citizens of the theocratic kingdom, masters and servants had become brothers together. . . . Thus, as seen in its widest application, only through its loyalty to God could Israel as a nation ever hope to be free and independent of other masters.
>
> A second feature of the Jubilee was that of the restitution of all real property. The purpose was to demonstrate that the earth is subject basically to God's law, and not to man's desires. . . . God's specific legislation concerned the inalienability of Israel's land titles. It required the reversion of all hereditary property to the family that originally possessed it and the reestablishment of the initial arrangement regarding God's division of the land. It did not teach either the socialistic economic theory that a person is entitled to ownership of goods on the basis of his need . . . or the free-enterprise system that allows an unlimited expansion of private property. On the contrary, it established a fixed title to the property assigned by God.[2]

What powerful messages these are—the Israelites were God's chosen children, all they possessed was God's, and only he could grant permanent title to the land. Truly, these messages, couched in the tradition of the jubilee year, reminded the people of Israel of their spiritual genealogy and their indebtedness to the Lord.

Second, Israel's celebrations and traditions also had a political component. These were times of uniting the tribes, of forming a closer union. Similarly, celebrations that commemorate important events in our native lands should receive our support and attention.

We declare in the twelfth article of faith, "We believe in being subject to kings, presidents, rulers, and magistrates, in obeying, honoring, and sustaining the law." We find that this counsel is continually needed in the Church today. Members of the Church should be committed to obeying and honoring the law of the land in which they live. We should be exemplary in our obedience to the laws of our local and national governments. As the Savior taught, we should render "unto Caesar the things which are Caesar's" so that the hearts of the leaders of nations are softened toward us, allowing us to render "unto God the things that are God's" (Matthew 22:21).

After the Savior's ministry, the apostles urged the Saints to be orderly and law abiding. Writing to Titus, Paul declared, "Put them in mind to be subject to principalities and powers, to obey magistrates, to be ready to every good work" (Titus 3:1).

As Church members, we live under many different national flags. How important it is that we understand our place and our position in the land in which we live! We should be familiar with the history, heritage, and laws that govern our land. In those countries that allow citizens the right to participate in the affairs of government, we should use our God-given agency and be actively engaged in supporting and defending the principles of truth, right, and freedom.

A third element of Israel's celebrations was their cultural impact on the people. Feasts and festivals were a time for sharing talents and accomplishments. They were a time of sharing practical knowledge associated with advancements in the arts and sciences.

Likewise, an important part of our pioneer heritage is an appreciation for all the cultural arts. Many of our pioneer forebears danced and sang as they crossed the plains. These simple entertainments helped them keep their spirits high in the face of tremendous hardship.

As the pioneers settled communities, they built theaters, organized bands and choruses, and sent artists on missions to gain the experience and training necessary to develop their talents fully. Certainly, we honor our pioneer heritage by placing unique and beautiful aspects of our culture at the center of our celebrations. And by so doing, are we not also praising the Lord through the beautiful creations of our hands and minds?

Finally, the celebrations and traditions of ancient Israel held deep social significance. They were a time of building a sense of community, a time to reaffirm the brotherhood and sisterhood shared by everyone, and a time for the bonding of families.

In a general conference of the Church in 1880, President John Taylor announced a jubilee year for the Church. Then he proposed to the members several ways to celebrate the jubilee year, ways that would draw the community of Saints more closely together. President Taylor said, "It occurred to me that we ought to do something, as they did in former times, to relieve those that are oppressed with debt, to assist those that are needy, to break the yoke off those that may feel themselves crowded upon, and to make it a time of general rejoicing."[3]

President Taylor then proposed the following:

1. That one-half of the debt of members to the Perpetual Emigration Fund be released. This amounted to more than $800, 000 in debt.

2. That the poor be released from the back tithing they owed. This represented nearly $76, 000.

3. That the Church raise a herd of one thousand milk cows to be distributed to the poor and needy. The Church was to contribute three hundred cows, and the rest would be gathered from the stakes of the Church.

4. That the Relief Society gather bushels of wheat to be loaned to the poor to be used as seed. Then after the harvest, the loan could be repaid, thus establishing a perpetual store of seed wheat. (Someone asked President Taylor if the wheat was to be loaned without interest. He replied, "Of course it is; we do not want any nonsense of that kind; it is the time of jubilee.")[4]

What a marvelous effect President Taylor's proposals must have had on the social structure of the Church. By recasting the traditions of ancient Israel in a way that responded to present-day needs, President Taylor showed the members of the Church how to be true latter-day Saints.

Celebrating important historical events and perpetuating traditions does not replace our study of history. Rather, it encourages it by building bridges between the present and the past and bringing relevance and interest to the study of history. When we celebrate, we remember. Sometimes we reenact what has gone on before us. When we honor traditions, we are more likely to retain the righteous spiritual, political, cultural, and social values our ancestors worked to pass along to their posterity.

I hope that as we continue to commemorate historical events and reclaim our traditions, we always celebrate with a purpose. I pray that we will make our celebrations more meaningful by reaffirming significant spiritual, political, cultural, and social values. As members of this great church, we share a rich heritage. We stand on the shoulders of the great people who preceded us and who were giants of faith, vision, and spirit. When we honor them and their many sacrifices, we preserve their achievements and the principles and values for which they stood.

We learn from ancient Israel that there is a place for commemorative events. Let us build in our families, communities, and nations those traditions that will consistently remind us of the Lord's eternal truths and of our forebears who preserved them for our day.

NOTES

1. *The International Dictionary of Thoughts,* comp. John P. Bradley et al. (Chicago: J. G. Ferguson Publishing Co., 1969), p. 362.

2. Geoffrey W. Bromley, ed., *The International Standard Bible Encyclopedia* (Grand Rapids, Mich.: William B. Eerdmans Publishing Co., 1968), 2:1142.

3. Conference Report, April 1880, p. 61.

4. Ibid., p. 64; see also pp. 62–63.

1 3

WORTHY TO ENTER

I HAVE ALWAYS been grateful I grew up in a community where the holy temple was a prominent feature. From almost anywhere in Cache Valley, I could look to the east, and there on the hill was the majestic Logan Temple. I have always appreciated its beauty, but more than that, I have appreciated its sacred purpose.

I also appreciated growing up in a home where my parents taught me what a great privilege it is to attend the temple. Some of my fondest memories are of watching my mother press temple clothes. It was done frequently in our home, and always with tender, loving care.

When my siblings and I were younger, we would anxiously anticipate (probably for the wrong reason) the times our parents went to the temple. Before Mother would leave, she would tie a few mints in the corner of her handkerchief so that if she had a problem with coughing while in the temple, she could quickly slip a mint into her mouth to avoid any disturbance during the session. She used the mints infrequently, so when she returned home from the temple, the mints were usually still in her handkerchief. Those of us who had been good while she and Father attended the temple were rewarded with a mint.

As I grew older, I gained a deeper appreciation of the blessings of temple attendance. My parents showed a special radiance as they returned from a temple session. The only way to describe their love for each other is to say it became more celestial after their visits to the temple.

At the time when I was approaching the age to be called to serve a full-time mission for the Church and to receive my temple endowments, my father was the bishop of our ward. Dad and I worked together frequently out in the backyard, hoeing the garden, cutting the hay, mending a fence, and milking a cow. He could have taken any of many occasions to give me a temple worthiness interview while we were out in the field or in the barn. But that is not the way my dad chose to approach this sacred event.

One day I received a call from my father at his office. He invited me to come to the chapel for a temple recommend interview. I thought it very strange at the time that he made the appointment in such a formal way. Mother had been notified and she helped me prepare for the interview. I dressed in a suit and tie before I went to meet with my father, the bishop, for my first temple recommend interview.

When I arrived at my father's office, the setting was very different than other times I had been there. There were no papers piled on the table, no reports. The desk was clear, and only the scriptures were in evidence as I walked in. Father greeted me and asked me to sit down. Then he commenced to interview me for my first temple recommend.

My father did not start the interview by asking questions. Instead he opened certain scriptures, and we read together. Then he commented about the scripture. I believe the first scripture we read was from the book of Moses, chapter 5, verse 5, when the Lord instructed Adam and Eve: "And he gave unto them commandments, that they should worship the Lord their God, and should offer the firstlings of their flocks, for an offering unto the Lord. And Adam was obedient unto the commandments of the Lord."

We discussed what it means to be obedient, to be familiar with the doctrines of the Church, not to belong to any apostate group or have leanings toward those who are unfriendly toward the gospel of our Lord and Savior. It was a lifting and learning experience to discuss the law of obedience.

The next scripture we turned to is found in First Corinthians, chapter 3: "Know ye not that ye are the temple of God, and that the Spirit of God dwelleth in you? If any man defile the temple of God, him shall God destroy; for the temple of God is holy, which temple ye are" (1 Corinthians 3:16–17).

Then we discussed what it means to be a temple of God, and how we defile that holy temple if we drink alcohol, use tobacco, or take any substance into our body that would cause us to be addicted and enslaved by repeated use.

This was followed by a discussion of moral cleanliness and the importance of keeping ourselves clean and not defiling our body through immoral acts. It was inspiring and humbling to listen to what it meant to be a temple of God.

The next scripture we turned to was section 119 of the Doctrine and Covenants, verse 4: "Those who have thus been tithed shall pay one-tenth of all their interest annually; and this shall be a standing law unto them forever, for my holy priesthood, saith the Lord."

This was followed by my father's own testimony of how tithing had continually blessed our family. Although times had not always been easy, the first part of all earnings he received from his legal·practice, the source of income, was deposited to the Church account in the bank where his office was located. It was a ritual with him. First, the tithing was paid, and then other expenses were met with what remained. His burning testimony of the law of tithing had a profound influence on me as I listened to his witness of how the Lord had blessed us as a family for his faithfulness in giving the Lord a tenth of his annual increase.

We then turned to section 21 of the Doctrine and Covenants:

> Behold, there shall be a record kept among you; and in it thou shalt be called a seer, a translator, a prophet, an apostle of Jesus Christ, an elder of the church through the will of God the Father, and the grace of your Lord Jesus Christ,
>
> Being inspired of the Holy Ghost to lay the foundation thereof, and to build it up unto the most holy faith. . . .
>
> Wherefore, meaning the church, thou shalt give heed unto all his words and commandments which he shall give unto you as he receiveth them, walking in all holiness before me. (D&C 21:1–2, 4)

We then had an opportunity to talk about what it means to sustain a prophet of the Lord. My father recounted some of his experiences with the prophets during his lifetime.

After these scriptures were read and discussed, the questions were posed to me: Do you live the Word of Wisdom? Are you morally clean? Are you obedient to the will of the Lord? Do you pay your tithes and offerings to the Lord? Do you sustain the prophet? All of these are familiar questions that we answer many times in our lives, whether we are renewing our temple recommends or being called to positions of responsibility in the Church.

After the interview was over and I had answered the questions to my father's satisfaction, he completed the temple recommend form and had me sign it. Then he signed it and got up from behind his desk. He threw his arms around me as he presented me with a little piece of paper signifying that I was worthy to enter the house of the Lord. Since that day, I have considered it a special, personal challenge in my life to always be able to sit in front of a priesthood leader and certify to him that I am worthy to hold a temple recommend and enter the Lord's house.

I don't think I have ever been more impressed with what a temple recommend means than when I served as a stake president. In the Boston stake, we had a dear widow who lived in one of the poorer sections of Boston. She had been struggling to sustain herself and sometimes even required a little of our assistance. She could not afford to move out of the apartment she had lived in for many years, but as the neighborhood deteriorated around her, it became almost a prison for her. When she went to the grocery store, she found the streets very unfriendly. One time she was knocked to the ground by an attacker who took her money.

After that terrifying experience, she requested that a priesthood bearer accompany her to the grocery store once a week. She had a system of unlocking the door for us when we arrived. We would rap on the door of her apartment, and we would hear her voice through the door, asking, "Who is it?" We would repeat our names, and then she would say, "Slide your temple recommend under the door so I can be certain it is you." After our recommends were pushed under the door, she would unlock the door and permit us to come in.

I have often thought about the significance of that experience. Because of all that is required to attain a temple recommend, a little piece of paper attests to our trustworthiness and integrity. That little piece of paper also opens the doors to our personal sanctification as we use it to draw closer to the Lord in his holy house.

The Lord declared in his instructions to Moses, "For behold, this is my work and my glory—to bring to pass the immortality and eternal life of man" (Moses 1:39). Immortality is to live forever in a resurrected state, with body and spirit inseparably connected. Immortality is a gift of God to his children through his grace. Eternal life is the name given to the kind of life our Heavenly Father lives. Only those who obey the fulness of the gospel law will inherit eternal life.

We have received this promise: "If you keep my commandments and endure to the end you shall have eternal life, which gift is the greatest of all the gifts of God" (D&C 14:7). Eternal life has no limits; we never stop in our eternal growth and increase. It comes to us only by entering into the new and everlasting covenant, being married for time and eternity by the power of the holy priesthood in the temple of the Lord.

May we always be worthy of holding a temple recommend. May it be one of our objectives in life to consistently and regularly sit before our priesthood leaders and declare our worthiness to receive this little piece of paper that, if we remain worthy to hold it, opens the door to the house of the Lord.

1 4

THE JOY OF HONEST LABOR

IN PROVERBS WE READ, "Train up a child in the way he should go: and when he is old, he will not depart from it"(Proverbs 22:6).

From the very beginning, one of the great challenges of life for parents has been the task of rearing children. This formidable responsibility seems destined to bring the greatest joys and some of the greatest sorrows of mortal life.

Every child, of course, is different, and what works for one may not elicit the desired response from another. However, I believe that second only to ensuring that each child receive an understanding of the gospel of Jesus Christ is teaching them the joy of honest labor.

I was taught this blessing by goodly parents. How grateful I am for a father who had the patience to teach me how to work. I remember that when I was only seven years old, we were remodeling our house, which involved tearing out the walls. In those days, two-by-sixes were used as studding. To the studs was nailed the lathe, and over the lathe came the plaster. When tearing out walls, the slats and the plaster were easy to knock off, but of course this left the nails in the two-by-sixes.

Each night after the workers had finished, I had the responsibility of gathering up the two-by-sixes and taking them to the back lawn, where there were two sawhorses. There I was to make a pile of the heavy boards and then, one at a time, put them on the sawhorses and with a crowbar remove all the nails. After the nails had been retrieved, I was told to straighten them. Finally, I threw the straightened nails into a large green bucket and stacked the two-by-sixes in a neat pile.

There was much in this project that was of value to me in my young life. First, I was taught to be productive, to be busily engaged, and not to waste my time in idleness.

From the very beginning, the Lord commanded Adam to till the earth and have dominion over the beasts of the field (see Moses 2:26), to eat his bread by the sweat of his face (see Moses 4:25). I am impressed at how often the scriptures admonish us to be productive in all of our labors, to cease to be idle. King Benjamin in his final address noted his example before the people: "I say unto you that as I have been suffered to spend my days in your service, even up to this time, and have not sought gold nor silver nor any manner of riches of you; . . . and even I, myself, have labored with mine own hands that I might serve you, and that ye should not be laden with taxes, and that there should nothing come upon you which was grievous to be borne—and of all these things which I have spoken, ye yourselves are witnesses this day" (Mosiah 2:12, 14).

The joy of honest labor is one of the great lessons we can teach our children. I am convinced that one of the reasons for the breakup of so many couples today is the failure of parents to teach and train sons in their responsibilities to provide and care for their families and to enjoy the challenge this responsibility brings. Many of us also have fallen short in instilling within our daughters the desire of bringing beauty and order into their homes through homemaking.

Oh, how essential it is that each child be taught early in life the joy that comes from starting and fashioning a job that is the workmanship of her or his own hands. Teach children the joy of honest labor. Provide a foundation that brings confidence and fulfillment to each life. "Happy is the man who has work he loves to do. Happy is the man who loves the work he has to do."[1]

Second, as a boy doing the job my father had assigned me, I was taught not to waste; to conserve resources where possible.

When the nails were pulled from them, the two-by-sixes could be used again—and we did use them.

I have always enjoyed reading some of the counsel that Brigham Young gave to the Saints in the early days of the Church. His counsel was always so practical. Listen to what he said about waste: "Pick up everything, let nothing go to waste. . . . Never consider that you have enough bread around to suffer your children to waste a crust or a crumb of it. . . . Remember it, do not waste anything, but take care of everything. . . . If you wish to get rich, save what you get. A fool can earn money; but it takes a wise man to save and dispose of it to his own advantage."[2]

I wonder what kind of signals we are sending to our children when we purchase homes that are status symbols. We waste space and resources when we buy a larger home than we need, a larger home than is practical for us to afford. We encumber ourselves with mortgages so large they require the income of both husband and wife to make payments. Then we build consumer debt to the point of completely absorbing all our disposable income, leaving no margin of safety for the rainy days that come into everyone's life. Such examples from parents only feed the philosophy of "I want it now" in their children. Lost to the next generation is the discipline associated with delayed gratification.

Some members of the Church have even arrived at the mistaken impression that after turning their ears away from the counsel of the prophets to avoid unnecessary debt, they can then turn to their bishops to bail them out of their foolishness. All the poor bishops can do is weep with them, help them move to more affordable housing, and suggest ways they can cut their losses.

As I reflect back on my life, I do not believe there was any difference in the degree of happiness I enjoyed when my two brothers and I shared a single bedroom as compared to the time when we had a home large enough for each of us to enjoy our own bedroom. Great lessons were taught me by wise parents who believed that what they spent should be dictated by what they could afford, not by what they wanted.

The third principle I learned from the experience with the

nails and the two-by-sixes is hard to put into words. I will never forget my consternation as I watched the workmen using new nails as they built the walls back up and completed the remodeling of our home. The pile of nails I had straightened and put in the green bucket grew and grew and was never used. I went to my father and said, "Wouldn't it be better to save the new nails and use the ones I have straightened?" I was proud of the work I had accomplished.

My father showed me something very important. He took a new nail and turned it at an odd angle to drive it into a board. He was able to drive it straight and true. Then he took one of the nails I had straightened so carefully and, turning it at the same odd angle, hit the old nail with the hammer. It soon bent and was impossible to drive into the board. So I learned that a used or bent nail is never as strong as a new one. But then why had my father asked me to straighten all those nails?

As a boy, I never remember receiving a satisfactory answer to that question. It was not until I had a son of my own that I started to understand. When my son was about three years old, I would take him out to the garden to help me weed. I assumed that he, being so low to the ground at the time, would have a real advantage at weeding. Unfortunately for my garden, he had a difficult time distinguishing between the weeds and the young plants.

I then tried Lee at milking a cow we jointly owned with a neighbor. He quickly developed the hand action of a fine milker, but sadly his aim was not very good. Whenever I checked on him, he was always surrounded by a white puddle and the milk bucket was nearly empty. He would look up at me and smile proudly, and my initial inclination to be angry would quickly disappear. But I was frustrated. I expected him to help me, but he only seemed to create more work.

It was at such a moment of frustration that I remembered straightening nails for my father, and I began to understand. Work is something more than its final end result. It is a discipline, something we must learn to do, and do well, before we can expect to receive tangible rewards for our labors. My father must have known that if he focused on the outcome of my labors, he would only become frustrated with how inadequately I performed. So he found tasks that were difficult and would challenge me, and thus he taught me the discipline of hard work. He was using the straightened nails not to remodel our home but to build my character.

The fourth thing I learned from my childhood work project was to finish the tasks I started. I was instructed to stack the used two-by-sixes neatly in a pile so the workmen could use them the next day. My work was never finished until this was done and the tools I had used were put away.

Let us also teach our children to see that their assigned work is carried to its completion and to take pride in what they have accomplished. There is a special satisfaction that comes from finishing a task, especially when it is the best work we know how to do.

These lessons instilled in me a sense of joy and appreciation for honest labor and prepared me for that time in my life when I would have the responsibility of providing for my own family. The principles I was being taught—of honest labor, conservation, discipline, and seeing a task to its completion—were basic to many of my successes in life. These lessons prepared me to meet the challenges of an ever-changing world.

Is this not the same lesson Paul preached? He declared, "Neither did we eat any man's bread for nought; but wrought with labour and travail night and day, that we might not be chargeable to any of you: not because we have not power, but to make ourselves an ensample unto you to follow us" (2 Thessalonians 3:8–9).

An event occurred in my life recently that again impressed upon me the blessings that accrue from good, early childhood training. When I arrived at the Salt Lake airport following a weekend assignment, I was delivered a note that one of my very best friends had passed away and that her funeral would be held in just an hour and a half in a community about fifty miles from the airport. I quickly found my car and started the drive to the funeral.

My friend had been my Primary teacher for three years when I was a Trail Builder. I had been nine, ten, and eleven years old when she taught me. As I drove to the funeral that morning, my mind was flooded with pleasant memories of my early childhood.

I especially remembered the powerful example of early childhood training. I remembered goodly parents who were always there to teach, inspire, and love and to give strong encouragement to help me chart the right course in my life. I remembered a kind aunt, who lived next door and who reinforced, with her words and example, the teachings of my parents.

Then I remembered my friend, Sister Call, who extended herself much beyond her call as a teacher. Her lessons included many field trips to teach us what life, labor, and the joy of friendships were all about. Her special way of weaving her lessons into our lives gave us an understanding of our personal worth.

As I drove along the highway, my heart was filled with overwhelming gratitude for parents, extended family, and Church members who had the patience, love, and concern to build a firm foundation in my life during those critical early years. All children need the same patience, love, and concern. The important lessons of life, lessons like the joy of honest labor, are taught by example. I leave this challenge with the adult members of the Church: May your examples be worthy of emulation by the children. If they are, I am confident that your examples will also be pleasing to the Lord.

NOTES

1. Author unknown, quoted by Adam S. Bennion, Conference Report, April 1955, p. 11.

2. *Discourses of Brigham Young*, sel. John A. Widtsoe (Salt Lake City: Deseret Book Co., 1954), p. 292.

1 5

BECOMING SELF-RELIANT

AFTER LEHI AND HIS FAMILY had wandered in the wilderness for eight years, they came to a land they called Bountiful because it was a place of much fruit and also wild honey. They came to a great sea, and they rejoiced unto the Lord because he had preserved them. After they had been in the land of Bountiful for the space of many days, the Lord spoke to Nephi and said, "Arise, and get thee into the mountain" (1 Nephi 17:7).

Nephi obeyed the Lord; he went into the mountain and prayed. And the Lord commanded Nephi, "Thou shalt construct a ship, after the manner which I shall show thee, that I may carry thy people across these waters" (1 Nephi 17:8).

Then Nephi asked, "Lord, whither shall I go that I may find ore to molten, that I may make tools to construct the ship after the manner which thou hast shown unto me?" (1 Nephi 17:9).

The Lord instructed Nephi where he could find ore, but then Nephi was left on his own to make the tools:

> And it came to pass that I, Nephi, did make a bellows wherewith to blow the fire, of the skins of beasts; and after I had made a bellows, that I might have wherewith to blow the fire, I did smite two stones together that I might make fire. . . .
> And it came to pass that I did make tools of the ore which I did molten out of the rock. (1 Nephi 17:11, 16)

This is one of the more interesting stories in the scriptures because it tells of an instance in which the Lord provided help but then stepped aside and allowed one of his sons to exercise his own initiative. I have sometimes wondered what would have happened if Nephi had asked the Lord for tools instead of a place to find ore to make the tools. I doubt the Lord would have honored Nephi's request. You see, the Lord knew that Nephi could make tools, and it is seldom that the Lord will do something for us that we can do for ourselves.

The Lord does help when we go to him in times of need, especially when we are committed to his work and responding to his will. But the Lord only helps those who are willing to help themselves. He expects his children to be self-reliant to the degree they can be.

Brigham Young instructed the Saints, "Instead of searching after what the Lord is going to do for us, let us inquire what we can do for ourselves."[1]

Independence and self-reliance are critical to our spiritual and temporal growth. Whenever we get into a situation that threatens our self-reliance, we will find our freedom threatened as well. If we increase our dependence on anything or anyone except the Lord, we will find an immediate decrease in our freedom to act. As President Heber J. Grant declared, "Nothing destroys the individuality of a man, a woman, or a child as much as the failure to be self-reliant."[2]

Self-reliance has become even more necessary in recent years. We live in a time of rapid change. Governments are rising and falling. Industries are booming and then, all too soon, becoming obsolete. New discoveries in science soon are overshadowed by newer discoveries. Unless we are continuously expanding our understanding and vision, we too will become out-of-date. Research tells us that individuals entering the labor market today will be forced to find three to five different career paths during their productive years.

What must we do to become more self-reliant? My parents established a family tradition in our home that was fun for me in my early years and has become even more meaningful as I have reflected back on it with the passing of years. On the first birthday of each child, the family would gather in the living room. In the center of the living room floor, our parents would place articles for the one-year-old child to select. The selection to be made might indicate an interest the child would pursue in life. The articles were a Bible, a child's bottle filled with milk, a toy, and a savings bank filled with coins. The child was placed on one side of the room and the family on the other side. Family members would encourage the child to crawl toward the objects and make a selection. This was all in fun, of course.

I was told that I selected the bank, and I went into finance as a profession. I watched my brother Ted select the scriptures, and he pursued law as his chosen profession. Over the years he has relied on the scriptures as a basis for his judgments. My youngest brother, Bob, was the well-rounded member of the family. He crawled over, sat down on the Bible, put the bottle of milk in his mouth, and held the toy in one hand and the bank in the other.

I now propose to you that in this entertaining family activity we can find some of the most fundamental principles of self-reliance. First, the scriptures represent our need for spiritual nourishment. In the scriptures the Lord reveals his will to his children. From the beginning of time, he has instructed his prophets to record his communications with them for the benefit of his children. The holy scriptures declare eternal values; they are the firm foundation on which we can build a successful mortal experience. We become more self-reliant when we study the holy scriptures, which teach the principles that provide a divine center to our lives here in mortality.

We should be comforted by the fact that we have the best text that has ever been written or ever will be written for our guide. We can turn to Second Kings, chapter 5, to learn about obedience. We can study the life of Job to learn integrity. King Benjamin's words in Mosiah chapter 2, verse 14, teach industry. The life of Joseph, as told in Genesis 39, tells us what to do when our standard of morality is being tested.

These are just a few examples of the lessons that can be learned from the holy scriptures. They are lessons that have stood the test of time. Our challenge is to make them come alive in the hearts and minds of our families as we assume the responsibility to teach them.

Second, the bottle filled with milk symbolizes the physical body's need for nourishment. Our Welfare Services program has taught us by using the spokes of a wheel to define the essential elements of temporal self-reliance. The elements contained in the wheel are education, physical health, employment, home storage, resource management, and social, emotional, and spiritual strength.

Recently my wife Barbara and I had an opportunity to visit with an eighty-year-old man who certainly demonstrates those elements in his life. He was born in a small Idaho town and worked long hours on the farm to finance his education. He spent his professional life teaching English and Spanish in a small high school. To set aside funds for missions and the education of his large family, he grew strawberry and raspberry crops to be picked and sold to local markets. This labor occupied his summers.

Because producing these fruits was so labor-intensive, few people had the ambition to grow them. Nevertheless, they were much-wanted crops. The demand was always there for as many berries as he could produce. He was never satisfied with current levels of productivity, so he studied new varieties of bushes in an attempt to find the best producers. His backyard was literally an experimental farm for testing the variety of bushes that produced the sweetest and most abundant fruit in his particular climate. His studies yielded increased productivity. The labor kept him in good physical health. The field of berries furnished automatic employment for his children each summer. The berries delivered to the market could be exchanged not only for cash but also for commodities to be used in the family's home storage. He managed his resources to build a beautiful home and supply the needs of his family.

This man loves to watch the Lord's system of multiplying and replenishing the earth, and he draws emotional and spiritual strength from his work. Now retired from active teaching, he continues to grow his berries, not for profit but for satisfaction. Six mornings each week during the berry harvest season, you will see him leading a parade of ten to twelve cars out of the city toward his berry patch. Families come to add to their home storage by picking the berries. I asked him the price per case if we supplied our own labor. He answered, "I don't know. My pay is seeing the look on people's faces as they leave the field holding the fruits of their labors in their arms."

I am convinced there are thousands of ways for families to build self-reliance by working together in productive pursuits. Perhaps a good family home evening discussion could produce some ideas to help make your family unit more temporally self-reliant.

Third, the toy I mentioned earlier represents the acquisition of things of the world. We are bombarded today with powerful media messages to "acquire now and pay later" in what are purported to be painless monthly installments. We live in an impatient world where everybody wants everything now. The acquisition of worldly goods seems to foster an appetite for more rather than any kind of lasting satisfaction.

Using our resources and worldly goods wisely and extending their life through preventive maintenance will help us become more self-reliant. I watched a young family move this summer, and I was intrigued by the labels on the boxes coming out of the storage room. They read, "Clothing—girls—2 years old," "Clothing—girls—3 years old," and so on up. Clearly, this family had a well-conceived plan for maximizing the usage of purchased items of clothing.

We live in a world blessed with so much abundance. Let us be certain that the resources with which we are blessed are never wasted.

Finally, the fourth item, the bank. It is a symbol of our financial well-being. I learned a great lesson early in my business career. My new boss called me into his office, and I could tell he had something on his mind. He said, "Give me a definition of interest." Of course, I reached back to my college training and gave him the definition I had learned from a textbook. He said, "No, no, no, that's not the one I want. You listen to this one: Them that under-stands it, earns it; and them that don't, pays it."

Now, it doesn't take a genius to understand that before you can collect interest you must first have some savings. Having a savings fund while continuing to increase one's standard of living requires understanding of one simple practice and then religiously applying it. After paying your tithing of ten percent to the Lord, pay yourself a predetermined amount directly into savings. That leaves you the balance of your income to budget for taxes, food, clothing, shelter, transportation, etc. It is amazing to me that so many people work all of their lives for the grocer, the landlord, the power company, the automobile salesman, and the bank and yet think so little of their own efforts that they pay themselves nothing.

Be prudent, wise, and conservative in your investment programs. It is by consistently and regularly adding to your investments that you will build your emergency and retirement savings. This will add to your progress in becoming self-reliant.

The principle of self-reliance is spiritual as well as temporal. It is not a doomsday program; it is something to be put into practice each and every day of our lives. Consider your ways. Develop a plan, and begin to work to become more self-reliant. The Lord does help those who have learned to help themselves.

NOTES

1. *Discourses of Brigham Young,* sel. John A. Widtsoe (Salt Lake City: Deseret Book Co., 1954), p. 293.

2. "Address," *Relief Society Magazine,* October 1937, p. 627.

1 6

"THEREFORE I WAS TAUGHT"

"I, NEPHI, having been born of goodly parents, therefore I was taught somewhat in all the learning of my father" (1 Nephi 1:1). What a different world this would be if the personal journals of each of our Father in Heaven's children could begin with a similar phrase—about having goodly parents and being taught by them.

We live in a unique time in history, a time when the Lord's gospel has been restored in its fulness. Our missionary force is increasing in quality and quantity; thus, the gospel is being taught in more languages, to more nations, and to greater numbers of listening ears than ever before. As wards and stakes are being established in most parts of the world, creative minds have been inspired to develop communication instruments that can bring the instructions of the prophets to the ears of these people. The good news of the gospel can now spread more rapidly to bring the hope of everlasting peace to the hearts and minds of all mankind.

One of the great messages of the gospel is the doctrine of the eternal nature of the family unit. We declare to the world the value and importance of family life, and we recognize that much of the confusion and difficulty existing in today's world can be traced to the deterioration of family life. Positive home experiences in which children are taught and trained by loving parents are diminishing.

Family life, with children and parents communicating together in study, play, and work, has been replaced by a microwaved individual dinner and an evening in front of the television set. In 1991 the National Association of Counties concluded that the lack of home influence had become a crisis in our nation, and it spent time in meetings discussing relevant concerns. The association identified five basic concepts that, if they were implemented, could increase every family's chances for success: first, strengthen relationships through family activities; second, establish reasonable rules and expectations; third, build self-esteem; fourth, set achievable goals; and fifth, periodically evaluate family strengths and needs.

Suddenly the urgent, warning voices of ancient and latter-day prophets have special relevance. Frequently and consistently, the prophets have encouraged and counseled us to be attentive to our own families. They have also encouraged the members of the Church to accelerate their missionary efforts to bring others to a knowledge of the eternal importance of the family unit.

In the very beginning, the Lord's instructions to Adam and Eve made clear their responsibilities as parents. The roles of the first parents were well defined. After Adam and Eve had received instructions from the Lord, we find them responding to his counsel:

> And in that day Adam blessed God and was filled, and began to prophesy concerning all the families of the earth, saying: Blessed be the name of God, for because of my transgression my eyes are opened, and in this life I shall have joy, and again in the flesh I shall see God.
>
> And Eve, his wife, heard all these things and was glad, saying: Were it not for our transgression we never should have had seed, and never should have known good and evil, and the joy of our redemption, and the eternal life which God giveth unto all the obedient.
>
> And Adam and Eve blessed the name of God, and they made all things known unto their sons and their daughters. (Moses 5:10–12)

From the very beginning, parents were expected to learn the ways of God; then they were given the responsibility to teach their children.

Latter-day revelations also admonish parents to teach and

train their children. In section 93 of the Doctrine and Covenants, the Lord chastised some of the brethren for not paying attention to their family responsibilities:

> I have commanded you to bring up your children in light and truth. . . .
>
> You have not taught your children light and truth, according to the commandments; and that wicked one hath power, as yet, over you, and this is the cause of your affliction.
>
> And now a commandment I give unto you—if you will be delivered you shall set in order your own house, for there are many things that are not right in your house. (D&C 93:40, 42–43)

Years ago, the Church established the family home evening program. Today, that program is woven into the fabric of many members' homes. Monday night has been set aside as an evening for the families to be together. No Church activities or social appointments are scheduled on this night. Great blessings are promised to those families who make a conscientious effort to hold a weekly family home evening.

President Lee once counseled us:

> Now [keep] in mind this; that when the full measure of Elijah's mission is understood, that the hearts of the children will be turned to the fathers, and the fathers to the children. It applies just as much on this side of the veil as it does on the other side of the veil. If we neglect our families here in having family home [evenings] and we fail in our responsibility here, how would heaven look if we lost some of those through our own neglect? Heaven would not be heaven until we have done everything we can to save those whom the Lord has sent through our lineage. So, the hearts of you fathers and mothers must be turned to your children right now, if you have the true spirit of Elijah, and not think that it applies merely to those who are beyond the veil. Let your hearts be turned to your children, and teach your children; but you must do it when they are young enough to be properly schooled. And if you are neglecting your family home evening, you are neglecting the beginning of the mission of Elijah just as certainly as if you were neglecting your research [in family histories].[1]

I've often thought of the happy times we had when our family was young and our children were at home. In my mind I have reviewed those early years and considered the changes I would make to our family organization if we could live that period again. There are two areas I would definitely improve if that privilege were granted me.

The first would be spending more time with my wife in family executive committee meetings in order to learn, communicate, plan, and organize our respective roles as parents.

The second wish would be to spend more family time. This includes more consistent, meaningful family home evenings.

The full burden of planning and preparing for family home evenings should not be left to the parents alone. The most successful ones I have witnessed are those where children assume an active role.

I call on you great children of the Primary, you deacons, teachers, and priests of the Aaronic Priesthood, and you young women of the Church to make major contributions to your family home evenings. In many homes you can be the conscience of the family. After all, you have the most to gain from the experience. Imagine how the knowledge and testimonies you gain from excellent family home evenings can add to the peace, security, and excellence of the world you will someday lead.

An example of how a righteous child can influence a family to do good occurred one year when our extended family had an outing on New Year's Eve. In order to have a real togetherness experience, we had arranged for a van so we could travel together. In the van were Grandpa and Grandma, my son, and his three older children. My son's wife had stayed at home with the younger children. I was driving, and my wife was seated next to me, acting as my navigator. From the rear of the van, I heard Audrey, my son's eldest child, counseling with her father. She was saying, "Dad, one of our family goals this year was to finish the Book of Mormon. This is the last day of the year. Why don't we complete it now so that we will reach our goal?"

What a special experience it was to listen to my son and his

three children each take turns reading aloud the final chapters of
Moroni to complete their goal of reading the entire Book of
Mormon. Remember, it was one of the children who made this
suggestion, not a parent.

The youth of the Church are a chosen generation, saved for
this critical time in the history of mankind. You have so much to
add to the growth and development of your families. I challenge
you to step forward with your special, youthful enthusiasm and
make the gospel really come alive in your homes. Remember the
counsel of President Joseph F. Smith:

> I would like my children, and all the children of Zion, to
> know that there is nothing in this world that is of so much value
> to them as the knowledge of the gospel as it has been restored
> to the earth in these latter days through the Prophet Joseph
> Smith. There is nothing that can compensate for its loss. There
> is nothing on earth that can compare with the excellency of the
> knowledge of Jesus Christ. Let, therefore, all the parents in Zion,
> look after their children, and teach them the principles of the
> gospel, and strive as far as possible to get them to do their
> duty—not mechanically, because they are urged to do it, but try
> to instill into the hearts of the children the spirit of truth and
> an abiding love for the gospel, that they may not only do their
> duty because it is pleasing to their parents, but because it is
> pleasing also to themselves.[2]

Family home evenings are for every family, whether a two-
parent home, a single-parent home, or the home of a single member. Along with my challenge to the youth of the Church, I
challenge the home teachers to encourage the families they visit to
hold regular and meaningful family home evenings.

President Ezra Taft Benson reminded the Saints of the necessity of holding family home evenings, and he listed the ingredients
that constitute a successful one. He said:

> Designed to strengthen and safeguard the family, the
> Church's [family] home evening program establishes one night
> each week that is to be set apart for fathers and mothers to
> gather their sons and daughters around them in the home.
> Prayer is offered, hymns and other songs are sung, scriptures are
> read, family topics are discussed, talent is displayed, principles

of the gospel are taught, and often games are played and home-made refreshments served.[3]

It is my hope that you will write down and consider each of these suggestions made by a latter-day prophet about what an effective family home evening should be.

President Benson continued:

> Now here are the blessings promised by a prophet of God for those who will hold weekly [family] home evenings: "If the Saints obey this counsel, we promise that great blessings will result. Love at home and obedience to parents will increase. Faith will be developed in the hearts of the youth of Israel, and they will gain power to combat the evil influences and temptations which beset them."[4]

Families of the Church, consider your ways. Are you holding regular and meaningful family home evenings? I give you my promise that this inspired program can be a shield and protection to you against the evils of our time and will bring you, individually and collectively, greater and more abundant joy.

NOTES

1. *Relief Society Courses of Study 1977–78* (Salt Lake City: The Church of Jesus Christ of Latter-day Saints, 1977), p. 2.

2. *Masterpieces of Latter-day Saint Leaders,* comp. N. B. Lundwall (Salt Lake City: Deseret Book Co., 1953), p. 78.

3. Official Report of the Philippine Islands Area Conference, 1975 (Salt Lake City: The Church of Jesus Christ of Latter-day Saints, 1975), p. 10.

4. Ibid.

"Choose the Right"

THE CHORUS OF James L. Townsend's stirring hymn text provides timeless advice about what to do when deciding between right and wrong. We should

> Choose the right! Choose the right!
> Let wisdom mark the way before.
> In its light, choose the right!
> And God will bless you evermore.[1]

On a recent trip to New Zealand, I met with a mission president who wore a lovely silver and turquoise tie tack with the inspiring CTR, or "Choose the Right," emblem etched on it. I had the impression that there must be a story behind his unique CTR pin. When I returned home, I wrote him a thank-you letter and asked him about his tie tack. I received this answer:

> You are very perceptive. Yes, there is a story behind the tie tack I'm wearing. . . . A few weeks before coming to New Zealand as a mission president, I was in the Kayenta Ward in Kayenta, Arizona. As I was saying some tender farewells to many of my Navajo friends, a remarkable young Navajo bishop gave me a big hug and then removed his tie tack and pinned it on my tie. As he did so, he asked me not to forget him.
>
> Now here in New Zealand, the last thing I do every morning as I dress for this great calling is to pin my tie tack with this beautiful silver and turquoise CTR emblem on my tie. I love it! I know it helps this old boilermaker make right choices throughout the day. I know also that it helps fulfill a prophetic

promise made to my wife and I from President Gordon B. Hinckley as he laid his hands on our heads and set us apart.

He said words to this effect: "You will have an instant bonding of love for every missionary in your mission." I can't tell you how many times that a missionary, during a visit, has said something like this: "President Gardner, I love your tie tack." And then he or she will show me their CTR ring.

I believe that Navajo bishop was inspired to give me the tie tack and that I make the right decision every day when I choose to wear it. And the blue and silver CTR pin is helping to bond me to a royal army of missionaries in the New Zealand Wellington Mission.

This letter from this special mission president has caused me to think about the "Choose the Right" motto of the Primary. Primary teachers instruct the youth of the Church in gospel principles that will help them always choose the right.

The Book of Mormon is filled with accounts of what happens to people who make both right and wrong choices. Let me refer to two examples:

During Alma's first year in the judgment seat, a large and strong man by the name of Nehor was brought before him to be judged. According to the scriptures, Nehor was going about among the people creating trouble and dissension:

> And he had gone about among the people, preaching to them that which he termed to be the word of God, bearing down against the church; declaring unto the people that every priest and teacher ought to become popular; and they ought not to labor with their hands, but that they ought to be supported by the people.
>
> And he also testified unto the people that all mankind should be saved at the last day, and that they need not fear nor tremble, but that they might lift up their heads and rejoice; for the Lord had created all men, and had also redeemed all men; and, in the end, all men should have eternal life. (Alma 1:3–4)

Nehor's words appealed to many of the people; they were easy words because they required neither obedience nor sacrifice. As we face many decisions in life, the easy and popular messages of the world will seem appealing. But when these worldly messages contradict gospel teachings and the still, small voice of the Spirit, we can be 100 percent confident they are wrong. Still, it will take great courage to choose the right.

Now the second example: In the land of Ammonihah, Amulek and Alma also found a people following false teachings. Amulek, speaking first, attempted to convert them again to the true and living gospel. Zeezrom, a man who was expert in the devices of the devil, challenged the teachings of Amulek. Zeezrom asked Amulek, "Shall [Jesus Christ] save his people in their sins?" Amulek answered and said, "I say unto you he shall not, for it is impossible for him to deny his word" (Alma 11:34).

Zeezrom taunted Amulek, but Amulek refused to waver in his faith. He chose the right by bearing testimony of the plan of redemption:

> And I say unto you again that he cannot save them in their sins; for I cannot deny his word, and he hath said that no unclean thing can inherit the kingdom of heaven; therefore, how can ye be saved, except ye inherit the kingdom of heaven? Therefore, ye cannot be saved in your sins. . . .
>
> And he shall come into the world to redeem his people; and he shall take upon him the transgressions of those who believe on his name; and these are they that shall have eternal life, and salvation cometh to none else.
>
> Therefore the wicked remain as though there had been no redemption made, except it be the loosing of the bands of death; for behold, the day cometh that all shall rise from the dead and stand before God, and be judged according to their works. (Alma 11:37, 40–41)

In this case, as it usually does, right prevailed. After considerable tribulation and a healing blessing, Zeezrom joined the Church.

The Prophet Joseph Smith taught: "Happiness is the object and design of our existence; and will be the end thereof, if we pursue the path that leads to it; and this path is virtue, uprightness, faithfulness, holiness, and keeping all the commandments of God."[2] True happiness comes only when we choose the right.

We live today in a world filled with choices. Television offers both good and bad. Bookstores are full of publications offering right and wrong. Because of the profanity, violence, and immorality that fill most movies, very few of them are worthy to be seen. Advertising is full of enticements to lead us to violate the Word of Wisdom. Music with its monotonous rhythms beats illicit thoughts into our heads.

Consider this counsel given by President Spencer W. Kimball:

> Now may I make a recommendation? Develop discipline of self so that, more and more, you do not have to decide and redecide what you will do when you are confronted with the same temptation time and time again. You need only to decide some things once. How great a blessing it is to be free of agonizing over and over again regarding a temptation. To do such is time-consuming and very risky.
>
> Likewise, my dear young friends, the positive things you will want to accomplish need be decided upon only once—like going on a mission and living worthily in order to get married in the temple—and then all other decisions related to these goals can fall into line. Otherwise, each consideration is risky, and each equivocation may result in error. There are some things Latter-day Saints do and other things we just don't do. The sooner you take a stand, the taller you will be![3]

To offset the worldly messages that entice us to choose the wrong, the Lord has blessed us with symbols of purity to keep us on the right course to choose the right. I was reminded of one of these symbols at a recent baptism of one of my granddaughters. In the little program that preceded her baptism, my granddaughter read this poem which had been written by her mother for this special occasion.

MY THREE WHITE DRESSES

My mom bought me a white dress,
Not red or pink or blue.
She said it was a special dress
Like very other few.

There has been just one before,
A dress now put away,
That I wore some time ago
Upon my blessing day.

As a little baby clothed
In my first white dress,
My dad held me in his arms,
There to name and bless.

So pure and clean was I just then,
With time to grow and learn
About the Father's plan for me.
My glory I must earn.

Now I've reached the age to judge
The wrong road from the right,
And I am here to be baptized
In this dress of white.

So once again I'm free from sin.
The path is clear to me.
I'll grasp the rod and hold on tight,
I vow with certainty.

Just as mud would stain my dress,
Sin would stain my soul.
The key is to repent or bleach,
For whiteness is my goal.

And if I try my very best,
Then richly blessed I'll be,
Wearing inside God's holy house
White dress number three.

So today I make this pledge:
I'll strive to choose the right
Through this sacred baptism ordinance
In my second dress of white.[4]

We are at a time in the history of the world when Satan is marshaling all his forces to lead people away from the strait and narrow path. Fortunately, most of the members of the Church are clear about who it is they will serve. Like Joshua of old, they proclaim, "As for me and my house, we will serve the Lord" (Joshua 24:15).

I hope and pray that you will have the courage to consistently choose the right. Moreover, I suggest that each of you find or create reminders to help you or your loved ones to choose the right when a choice is placed before you. There is power in a tie tack, a CTR ring, or a white dress hanging in the closet if we associate them with our desires for purity and righteousness. Even more important than physical reminders is the conviction deep down in our hearts to live the kind of life that will lead to right choices, not only for peace and happiness right now but also for eternity. All of us have been promised that we will receive everlasting happiness if we consistently choose the right.

NOTES

1. *Hymns,* no. 239.

2. Joseph Smith, *History of The Church of Jesus Christ of Latter-day Saints,* 2d ed. rev., ed. B. H. Roberts (Salt Lake City: The Church of Jesus Christ of Latter-day Saints, 1932–51), 5:134–35.

3. *President Kimball Speaks Out* (Salt Lake City: Deseret Book Co., 1981), p. 94.

4. Linda Gay Perry Nelson, 1993.

Thy Speech Reveals Thee

Peter is a character in the New Testament who has always held a special fascination for me. He had to struggle so hard to overcome the things of the world and prepare himself to be a true witness and teacher of the gospel of Jesus Christ. There is an intriguing lesson to be learned from the interactions between the Savior and Peter during the final hours before the Savior's trial and crucifixion.

The scriptures tell us that the Savior and his disciples met together for the Last Supper, then sang a hymn and went out to the Mount of Olives. It is recorded:

> Then saith Jesus unto them, All ye shall be offended because of me this night: for it is written, I will smite the shepherd, and the sheep of the flock shall be scattered abroad.
>
> But after I am risen again, I will go before you into Galilee.
>
> Peter answered and said unto him, Though all men shall be offended because of thee, yet will I never be offended.
>
> Jesus said unto him, Verily I say unto thee, That this night, before the cock crow, thou shalt deny me thrice.
>
> Peter said unto him, Though I should die with thee, yet will I not deny thee. (Matthew 26:31–35)

Peter drew strength from the Savior, and his courage was evident when he was in the company of the Savior. If Peter could have seen the Savior, perhaps made eye contact with him, he may not have denied him thrice. But Peter was alone and therefore more vulnerable to fear.

Out of this love for the Savior, Peter followed him to the palace of Caiaphas. As Peter sat outside the palace, he was approached and questioned first by a servant girl, then by another woman (see Matthew 26:69–72). He denied the Savior twice. Then individuals from a group of curious onlookers said to Peter:

> Surely thou also art one of them; for thy speech bewrayeth thee.
> Then began he to curse and to swear, saying, I know not the man. And immediately the cock crew.
> And Peter remembered the word of Jesus, which said unto him, Before the cock crow, thou shalt deny me thrice. And he went out, and wept bitterly. (Matthew 26:73–75)

In verse 73, the Greek translation of "bewrayeth thee" is "reveals you." Just as a passport photo, a signature, or a thumbprint identifies each of us, our speech reveals who we are, as well as where and how we were raised. As with Peter, our speech reveals us. Others can classify us, place us in certain categories, after hearing us speak only a few words.

My Fair Lady has always been one of my favorite musicals. In the opening scene, Professor Henry Higgins brags to a colleague that he can identify a person's station in life and their country of origin by the way they speak. As you remember, Professor Higgins accepts the challenge of taking a lowly street person, a young lady named Eliza Doolittle, and, through demanding preparation and training, refining her speech so she may be mistaken for a woman of nobility. The many struggles encountered by Professor Higgins and Eliza Doolittle show that changing speech patterns is nearly as difficult as changing lifestyle. Moreover, changes in speech patterns often invoke changes of lifestyle.

The way we speak reflects the kind of person we are, exposing our background and our way of life. It describes our thinking, as well as our inner feelings. Unfortunately, in many people's minds, profanity and vulgarity are socially more acceptable than they used to be. This concerning trend seems to be influenced by what we watch on television and at the movies. Many of these so-called forms of entertainment are filled with language that can only defile the minds of men and women.

My wife Barbara had a birthday some time ago. I suggested to her that we celebrate this event by going to a movie together. We scanned the movie advertisements in the newspaper to find one that would be comfortable for us to watch. We chose a movie with a PG rating, assuming it would not offend us. Unfortunately, we were wrong. Just a few minutes into the movie, we got up and left. We could not tolerate the foul language. As I left the movie theater, I felt embarrassed. I did not want anyone to see me coming out of a movie with such vulgar language.

An experience in my life taught me that using the wrong word can disappoint even people whose standards are lower than your own. I was in boot camp in the U.S. Marine Corps during World War II. Of course, the language of my fellow marines was not what anyone would describe as exemplary. Being a recently returned missionary, however, I determined that I needed to be an example. I endeavored to keep from saying even the simplest and most common of swearwords.

One day, I was firing at the rifle range to earn my final score. I had done well in the 100-, 200-, and 300-yard positions. Now I was back at the 500-yard position. All I needed was a reasonable score, and I would make Expert Rifleman. I was excited. *If my buddies do as well as I have, we should have the top platoon,* I thought. But I tensed up, and on my first shot I threw my shoulder into the rifle. Of course, the flag waved—I had missed the target. And likewise, I missed the opportunity of being named an Expert Rifleman.

At that moment of frustration and disappointment, out of my mouth came a four-letter word that I had resolved never to use. Much to my chagrin, everyone at the range stopped firing. They turned and looked at me with their mouths open in astonishment. Any other marine firing from that position that day could have used the word I used without anyone paying attention. Because I had determined that I would carry the standards of the mission field into the Marine Corps, everyone was disappointed when I allowed my words to misrepresent me.

People from all ages have been strong in their criticism of those who use vulgarity and profanity in their speech. It was S. H. Cox who said, "Of all the dark catalogue of sins, there is not one more vile and execrable than profaneness. It commonly does, and loves to cluster with other sins; and he who can look up and insult his Maker to his face, needs but little improvement in guilt to make him a finished devil."[1]

Shakespeare said, "Ill deeds are doubled with an evil word."[2]

George Washington observed, "The foolish and wicked practice of profane cursing and swearing is a vice so mean and low, that every person of sense and character detests and despises it."[3]

Church leaders have implored and pleaded with the Saints to use the right language. President Spencer W. Kimball said, "When we go to places of entertainment and mingle among people, we are shocked at the blasphemy that seems to be acceptable among them. The commandment says, 'Thou shalt not take the name of the Lord thy God in vain.' (Exodus 20:7.) Except in prayers and proper sermons, we must not use the name of the Lord. Blasphemy used to be a crime punishable by heavy fines. Profanity is the effort of a feeble brain to express itself forcibly."[4]

President Stephen L Richards wrote, "How regrettable it is that man, seemingly oblivious to this honorable and sacred relationship, should profane his [God's] holy name and blaspheme Christ. Do you think that a son can damn his father and love him?"[5]

The Savior himself said, "Not that which goeth into the mouth defileth a man; but that which cometh out of the mouth, this defileth a man" (Matthew 15:11).

Many times in our effort to control our speech, we employ other words as substitutes. Sometimes, however, these substitute worlds are so close to vulgar and profane words that they remind the people who hear them of the words we want to avoid. I have been appalled at times as I have listened to missionaries give their homecoming addresses and have heard some of the phrases, sentences, or words they have learned in the mission field. It was obvious to me and everyone else that these words were really substitutes for profanity and vulgarity. The use of these words demonstrated the missionary's inability to master a proper vocabulary and gave the wrong impression of what the missionary had been doing in the mission field.

To anyone who uses profanity or vulgarity and would like to remove the habit, could I offer this suggestion? First, make the commitment to erase such words from your vocabulary. Next, if you slip and say a swearword or a substitute word, mentally reconstruct the sentence without the offensive word and repeat the new sentence aloud. Eventually you will learn to speak in a way that will reveal you for what you are: a true follower of Christ.

I think the instructions Paul gave to the Ephesians apply to all of us: "Let no corrupt communication proceed out of your mouth, but that which is good to the use of edifying, that it may minister grace unto the hearers. And grieve not the holy Spirit of God, whereby ye are sealed unto the day of redemption (Ephesians 4:29–30).

I encourage you to have the resolve, discipline, and courage to keep your words clean and wholesome. Improve your speech, and others will immediately recognize your commitment to serve the Lord.

In conclusion, let me quote the words of him we serve. The Savior said, "A good man out of the good treasure of his heart bringeth forth that which is good; and an evil man out of the evil treasure of his heart bringeth forth that which is evil: for of the abundance of the heart his mouth speaketh" (Luke 6:45).

NOTES

1. *The New Dictionary of Thoughts,* comp. Tyron Edwards (n.p.: Standard Book Co., 1959), p. 521.

2. Ibid.

3. Ibid.

4. Conference Report, October 1974, p. 7.

5. *Where Is Wisdom?* (Salt Lake City: Deseret Book Co., 1955), p. 238.

Heed the Prophet's Voice

Aᴘʀɪʟ 6, 1830, is a significant date for Latter-day Saints. It is the day The Church of Jesus Christ of Latter-day Saints was organized. The translation and printing of the Book of Mormon had been completed, the priesthood had been restored, and the Lord directed that his church should again be organized here on the earth.

Prospective members of the Church gathered at the home of Peter Whitmer, Sr., in Fayette, New York, for this special occasion. The meeting was simple. Joseph Smith, then twenty-four years of age, called the group to order and designated five associates to join him in satisfying New York's legal requirements for the incorporation of a religious society. After kneeling in solemn prayer, Joseph Smith proposed that he and Oliver Cowdery be called as teachers and spiritual advisers to the newly organized Church. All raised their right arms to the square, and the pattern of sustaining Church leadership was established.

At that meeting, the revelation contained in section 21 of the Doctrine and Covenants was received. In that revelation, the Lord said to the Prophet Joseph Smith, "Behold, there shall be a record kept among you; and in it thou shalt be called a seer, a translator, a prophet, an apostle of Jesus Christ, an elder of the church through the will of God the Father, and the grace of your Lord Jesus Christ, being inspired of the Holy Ghost to lay the foundation thereof, and to build it up unto the most holy faith" (D&C 21:1–2).

I would like to use this scripture as a stepping-stone to

consider what it means to sustain the president of the Church as a seer and prophet.

First is the title of seer. Moses, Samuel, Isaiah, Ezekiel, and many others were seers. They were seers because they were blessed with a clearer vision of divine glory and power than other mortals.

Perhaps the best description we have of a seer is in the Book of Mormon account of Ammon's arrival in the land of Lehi-Nephi. There was much rejoicing in the land over the arrival of Ammon. King Limhi addressed his people and called on Ammon to rehearse what had happened to their brethren since they had been separated. Then King Limhi sent his people to their homes and requested that the plates containing a record of his people from the time they had left Zarahemla be brought before Ammon that he might read them. As soon as Ammon had read the record, the king inquired of him to know if he could interpret languages from other records he had in his possession, and Ammon told him he could not. Then Ammon said:

> I can assuredly tell thee, O king, of a man that can translate the records; for he has wherewith that he can look, and translate all records that are of ancient date; and it is a gift from God. . . .
>
> And the king said that a seer is greater than a prophet.
>
> And Ammon said that a seer is a revelator and a prophet also; and a gift which is greater can no man have, except he should possess the power of God, which no man can; yet a man may have great power given him from God.
>
> But a seer can know of things which are past, and also of things which are to come, and by them shall all things be revealed, or, rather, shall secret things be made manifest, and hidden things shall come to light, and things which are not known shall be made known by them, and also things shall be made known by them which otherwise could not be known. (Mosiah 8:13, 15–17)

Ammon explains that a seer is both a revelator and a prophet, so he is greater than a prophet. This may explain why through the ages of history there have been more prophets than seers. Joseph

Smith, of course, was the great seer of the latter days. He was acting in the role of seer when he translated the Book of Mormon.

What does it mean to be a prophet? The word *prophet* comes from a word in the Greek language that means "inspired teacher."[1] In Hebrew, the word for prophet means "one who announces or brings a message from God." According to Elder John A. Widtsoe:

> A prophet is a teacher. That is the essential meaning of the word. He teaches the body of truth, the gospel, revealed by the Lord to man; and under inspiration explains it to the understanding of the people. He is an expounder of truth. Moreover, he shows that the way to human happiness is through obedience to God's law. He calls to repentance those who wander away from the truth. He becomes a warrior for the consummation of the Lord's purposes with respect to the human family. The purpose of his life is to uphold the Lord's plan of salvation. All this he does by close communion with the Lord, until he is "full of power by the spirit of the Lord."[2]

While my father attended LDS High School he worked and lived in the home of President Joseph F. Smith. In his life history, Father wrote this of President Smith:

> Most great men that I have known have been deflated by intimate contact. Not so with the prophet Joseph F. Smith. Each common every day act added inches to his greatness. To me he was prophet even while washing his hands or untying his shoes.

My father tells of one experience in which the prophet taught him a practical lesson late one night as he entered the Beehive House. Again I quote from my father's life history:

> I walked with guarded steps through the office, then into the private study to the door at the foot of the steps that led to my bedroom. But the door would not open. I pushed and I pushed to no avail. Finally, I gave up and went back to a rug that I had noticed in the hall with the intention of sleeping there until morning.
>
> In the darkness I bumped against another partially opened door and the collision awakened the prophet. He turned on the light and, seeing who it was, came down the stairway and inquired concerning my difficulty.
>
> "The door is locked that leads to my room," I explained. He

went to the door and pulled instead of pushed and the door opened. Had he been disturbed by my foolish blunder I would not have been surprised, for I had robbed him of a precious night's sleep by a thoughtless act. He only smiled and stopped to inquire of a strange stable boy what I had stumbled into. I pointed to the half open door at the other end of the hall.

"Let me show you something." He took time at midnight to explain, "When in the dark never go groping with hands parted and outstretched, that permits doors to get by your guard and hit you. Keep your arms in front, but hands together, then you will feel with your hands and not your head." I thanked him and moved to my quarters. He waited until I reached the rear stairway and then he retired.

Isn't a prophet someone who teaches us to open doors we thought we could not open ourselves—doors to greater light and truth? Isn't a prophet like a pair of hands clasped together in front of the body of the Church helping the members navigate through the dark corridors of the world? Isn't a prophet someone who watches and waits for us patiently while we get to where we need to be?

Never has there been a time when the written and spoken word can descend upon us from so many different sources. Through the media, we find analysts analyzing the analysts, almost overwhelming us with opinions and diverging views.

What a comfort it is to know that the Lord continues to keep a channel of communication open to His children through the prophet! What a blessing it is to know we have a voice we can trust to declare the will of the Lord! As the prophet Amos taught: "Surely the Lord God will do nothing, but he revealeth his secret unto his servants the prophets" (Amos 3:7).

The Lord surely understood the need to keep his doctrine pure and to trust its interpretation to only one source. Of course, we are all admonished to study and gain as much knowledge as we can possibly obtain in this life. We are encouraged to discuss and exchange ideas one with another to further our understanding. However, the Lord has only one source for the declaration of his basic fundamental doctrines. Even as General Authorities of the Church, our instructions are clear: "In order to preserve the uniformity of doctrinal and policy interpretation, you are asked to refer to the Office of the First Presidency for consideration and response to any doctrinal or policy questions which are not clearly defined in the scriptures or in the *General Handbook of Instructions.*"

In this way, conflict and confusion and differing opinions are eliminated.

President Brigham Young assured us that we can have complete confidence in the prophets. He said, "The Lord Almighty leads this Church, and he will never suffer you to be led astray if you are found doing your duty. You may go home and sleep as sweetly as a babe in its mother's arms, as to any danger of your leaders leading you astray, for if they should try to do so the Lord would quickly sweep them from the earth. Your leaders are trying to live their religion as far as they are capable of doing so."[3]

When I was just seven years old, I had my first experience meeting a prophet of God. President Heber J. Grant came to our home for dinner before he dedicated our new ward chapel. We were living in Logan at the time, and my father was the bishop. Of course, as children we were not allowed to eat dinner with the prophet. Our manners were not ready for that type of company. So my sisters, brothers, and I took turns looking through the key-hole in the kitchen to watch President Grant eat.

After dinner, before my mother had finished cleaning up the kitchen, she sent me to the chapel to save a seat for her. She soon arrived, and we waited together for the meeting to start. When the time came to start the meeting, however, President Grant and my father had still not arrived. My mother looked worried. She told me both President Grant and my father had decided to take a short nap before the meeting. She wondered if they had overslept. Finally she told me, "You'd better run home and wake them up."

I ran home as fast as I could. I chose to wake my father first, hoping he would wake up the prophet and tell him they were late for the meeting. My father, however, was too embarrassed to awaken the prophet. He asked me to go into the adjoining bedroom and wake up President Grant.

Hesitantly, I approached President Grant. Gently I shook his shoulder. Meekly I told the prophet of the Lord that he had over-slept. I remember how kind and considerate he was to me during those few minutes we were alone together. Instead of rushing, he took time to have me sit on the bed with him. He patted my shoulder and thanked me for the small service I provided. He asked me about my relationship with my father, mother, sisters, and brothers. Finally, we stood up and made our way to the chapel. I will never forget the experience of sitting alongside the prophet of God with his arm around my shoulder. I was just a boy of seven, but I recognized a prophet's voice. The thought never occurred to me to question any of his kind counsel. I drank in every word.

During my lifetime, I have been blessed on several occasions by close, intimate contact with the Lord's chosen servant, the prophet. I recognize that many members of the Church will never have the opportunity to meet the prophet face-to-face. Nevertheless, we can all drink in the prophet's words. We can all take to heart his wise counsel. We can all be touched by the spirit of the prophet of God.

The members of this church are blessed to have a prophet, the Lord's mouthpiece, at its head. We can trust the prophet never to lead the members of the Church astray. We should listen, consider, and follow his counsel to us. As President J. Reuben Clark observed, "We do not lack a prophet; what we lack is a listening ear by the people and a determination to live as God has commanded."[4] I pray that all the members of the Church will recognize that there is safety when we follow the prophet and strictly heed his voice.

NOTES

1. Daniel H. Ludlow, ed., *Encyclopedia of Mormonism* (New York: Macmillan, 1992), 3:1164.

2. *Evidences and Reconciliations,* arr. G. Homer Durham (Salt Lake City: Bookcraft, 1960), p. 257.

3. *Discourses of Brigham Young,* sel. John A. Widtsoe (Salt Lake City: Deseret Book Co., 1954), p. 137.

4. Conference Report, October 1948, p. 80.

2 0
....

"THE PEACEABLE FOLLOWERS OF CHRIST"

COLONEL THOMAS L. KANE, who was not a member of the Church,
spoke to the Historical Society of Philadelphia, Pennsylvania. He
told the audience that during his travels a few years before, he had
passed through a very unusual city, Nauvoo, Illinois, on the banks
of the Mississippi River. He explained that after traveling up the
river for some time, he left the steamer and began to travel on land
because of the rapids in the river.

While on the road, he had seen only unimproved country
where idlers and outlaws had settled. Then he saw Nauvoo. Let me
quote Colonel Kane:

> I was descending the last hillside upon my journey, when a
> landscape in delightful contrast broke upon my view. Half
> encircled by a bend of the river, a beautiful city lay glittering in
> the fresh morning sun. Its bright new dwellings [were] set in
> cool green gardens ranging up around a stately dome-shaped
> hill, which was crowned by a noble marble edifice, whose high
> tapering spire was radiant with white and gold. The city
> appeared to cover several miles, and beyond it, in the back-
> grounds, there rolled off a fair country chequered by the care-
> ful lines of fruitful husbandry. The unmistakable marks of
> industry, enterprise and educated wealth everywhere, made the
> scene one of singular and most striking beauty. . . . No one met
> me there. I looked and saw no one. I could hear no one move,
> though the quiet everywhere was such that I heard the flies buzz
> and the water ripples break against the shallow beach. I walked
> through the solitary streets. The town lay as in a dream, under
> some deadening spell of loneliness, from which I almost feared

to wake it, for plainly it had not slept long. There was no grass growing up in the paved ways, rains had not entirely washed away the prints of dusty footsteps, yet I went about unchecked. I went into empty workshops, rope walks and smithies. The spinner's wheel was idle, the carpenter had gone from his work bench and shavings, his unfinished sash and casings, fresh bark was in the tanner's vat, and fresh chopped light wood stood piled against the baker's oven. The blacksmith's shop was cold; but his coal heap and ladling pool and crooked water horn were all there, as if he had just gone for a holiday. . . .

Fields upon fields of heavy headed yellow grain lay rotting ungathered upon the ground. No one was at hand to take in their rich harvest.[1]

Colonel Kane could not understand why such a beautiful city had been abandoned. He was unaware that the Saints had been driven from their city by the mobs. His curiosity caused him to search for the people who had left the city. When he found them, he observed that even though they were suffering and dying of hunger and exposure, they were peaceful and wholesome. He asked, "Why were such harmless people so persecuted?"

In some ways the situation has not changed a great deal today. The Church still faces some situations that, in many ways, are similar to the Nauvoo period. There is not, of course, the same degree of antagonism manifest against us as in our early history. But we still must wonder, as Colonel Kane did, why certain individuals and groups feel it is their duty to persecute the Church, both its doctrine and its people.

Mormon began his great speech about faith, hope, and charity by addressing the members of the Church as "the peaceable followers of Christ" (Moroni 7:3). What does it mean to be a peaceable follower of Christ? Some of our more profound examples are our pioneer ancestors, who after enduring continuous persecution turned the other cheek instead of fighting back. Of course, we also have stories in Church history of individuals and groups who became vindictive and sought revenge from the enemies of the Church. The reason these stories are remembered is that they stand out in sharp contrast against the standard, peaceful responses of our pioneer forefathers. Aggression and revenge were the exceptions, not the rule.

The story of the people of Anti-Nephi-Lehi provides a scriptural account of what it means to become a peaceable follower of Christ. The people of Anti-Nephi-Lehi were the Lamanite converts of Ammon and his brethren. They came from seven lands and cities and numbered in the many thousands (see chapter head, Alma 23). Once they were converted to the gospel of Jesus Christ, the Anti-Nephi-Lehies covenanted to never return to the bloodthirsty traditions of their forebears. Even when their Lamanite brethren, aroused by the wicked Amalekites and Amulonites, prepared to make war against them, the Anti-Nephi-Lehies refused to lift up their weapons to defend themselves:

> Now when Ammon and his brethren and all those who had come up with him saw the preparations of the Lamanites to destroy their brethren, they came forth to the land of Midian, and there Ammon met all his brethren; and from thence they came to the land of Ishmael that they might hold a council with Lamoni and also with his brother Anti-Nephi-Lehi, what they should do to defend themselves against the Lamanites.
>
> Now there was not one soul among all the people who had been converted unto the Lord that would take up arms against their brethren; nay, they would not even make any preparations for war; yea, and also their king commanded them that they should not. (Alma 24:5–6)

The king of the Anti-Nephi-Lehies instructed his people to bury their weapons deep in the ground that they might not be tempted to use them when their Lamanite brethren came to do battle against them. The people followed their king's instructions, viewing their actions as "a testimony to God, and also to men, that they never would use weapons again for the shedding of man's blood" (Alma 24:18). When the Lamanites attacked, the Anti-Nephi-Lehies "went out to meet them, and prostrated themselves" on the ground before their attackers (Alma 24:21). The Lamanites killed a thousand and five of the Anti-Nephi-Lehies before the slaughter stopped. Why did the slaughter stop, and what were its consequences? From the account in Alma we learn the answers to these questions:

> Now when the Lamanites saw this they did forbear from slaying them; and there were many whose hearts had swollen in them for those of their brethren who had fallen under the sword, for they repented of the things which they had done.
>
> And it came to pass that they threw down their weapons of war, and they would not take them again, for they were stung for the murders which they had committed; and they came down even as their brethren, relying upon the mercies of those whose arms were lifted to slay them.
>
> And it came to pass that the people of God were joined that day by more than the number who had been slain; and those who had been slain were righteous people, therefore we have no reason to doubt but what they were saved. (Alma 24:24–26)

The message of this story is not that all members of the Church should conscientiously object to war. There is also a Book of Mormon story about Captain Moroni raising the "title of liberty" as the leader of the true believers in Christ (see Alma 46:11–14). Moroni made impassioned speeches and wrote spirited letters to his Nephite brethren about protecting their liberty, lands, wives, children, and peace (see Alma 48:10). It was the Anti-Nephi-Lehies' unique history that caused them to make a unique covenant with the Lord that they felt an obligation to honor. When they honored their covenant they were blessed, and their brethren, the Lamanites, were also blessed.

While the message of the story is not to insist on universal pacifism, we do learn that by not returning aggressions from others we can have a profound effect on them. Literally, we can change their hearts when we follow Christ's example and turn the other cheek. Our examples as peaceable followers of Christ inspire others to follow him.

Stephen, one of the "seven men of honest report" chosen to assist the ancient apostles, was a man filled with the Holy Ghost, a man who also followed Christ's example of peace (see Acts 6:3, 5). His last words, as he was being stoned to death by the Jews, were "Lord, lay not this sin on their charge" (Acts 7:60). Stephen's words are reminiscent of Christ's appeal while hanging from the cross: "Father, forgive them; for they know not what they do" (Luke 23:34).

Recently, I read a book by Robert Coles, a pediatrician and child psychologist, with an intriguing title: *The Call of Service.* He told the story of a six-year-old girl named Tessie, who was one of the three black children involved in the desegregation of McDonogh 19 School in New Orleans during the fall of 1961. Every day the federal marshals would arrive at Tessie's house at about 8:00 A.M. to escort her to school. Walking into school, she was forced to pass by a mob of angry parents and children, who yelled obscenities and threats at her. Robert Coles, at the time involved in a study on psychoanalytic threatening, provided emotional support to Tessie. He was intrigued by her stoic courage and had a great desire to understand it.

According to Robert Coles, at the heart of the passive resistance movement for racial equality was Christian faith and love. On a day when Tessie's resolve was weakening, her maternal grandmother lectured her about her service. She said, "You belong in that McDonogh School, and there will be a day when everyone knows that, even those poor folks—Lord, I pray for them!—those poor, poor folks who are out there shouting their heads off at you. You're one of the Lord's people; He's put His Hand on you. He's given a call to you, a call to service—in His name!"[2]

Later, Coles asked Tessie if she knew what her grandmother had meant. Tessie replied, "If you just keep your eyes on what you're supposed to be doing, then you'll get there—to where you want to go. The marshals say, 'Don't look at them; just walk with your head up high, and you're looking straight ahead.' My granny says that there's God, He's looking too, and I should remember that it's a help to Him to do this, what I'm doing; and if you serve Him, then that's important. So I keep trying."[3]

For Tessie, service meant service to Heavenly Father. Her call from Heavenly Father was to change the hearts of her enemies in this battle over racial equality. It was her faith in God and in the importance of her call to serve that sustained her through several months of the bitterest of trials. She could do as the Savior instructed—"Love your enemies, bless them that curse you, do good to them that hate you, and pray for them which despitefully use you, and persecute you" (Matthew 5:44)—because, in her words, "if I can help the good Lord and do a good job, then it'll all be okay, and I won't be wasting my time."[4]

Not only did Tessie's service bless the lives of blacks who lived in the South; it also blessed the lives of their white enemies. Two months into the ordeal, a woman, one of the protestors, wrote Tessie an anonymous letter. It read:

> Dear little girl,
>
> I stand there with them and sometimes I've shouted, along with everyone else, but I feel sorry for you, and I wish all this trouble will end, soon. You're good to smile at us, like you do sometimes, and I want you to know I'm praying this will be over, and my kids will soon be back in school with you and the other two.[5]

Tessie's love for her enemies had penetrated a milieu of hate and redefined the relationship between enemies. The woman who wrote the letter was the first of many protestors to realize that they could not win a battle against a six-year-old girl who refused to fight back.

The Anti-Nephi-Lehies, Stephen, and young Tessie are all examples of what it means and what it takes to become one of "the peaceable followers of Christ." At the heart of the matter is the heart—a heart somehow changed by the love of God and an understanding that even our enemies are our brothers and sisters and, therefore, part of his eternal family.

The path to becoming a peaceable follower of Christ is long and difficult, requiring innumerable changes. I hope these examples will help keep your eyes pointed in the right direction so you can get where you want to go. In conclusion, let me offer a little suggestion to help fortify your resolve.

Sometimes in our enthusiasm for the gospel, we cast our pearls indiscriminately, and we might even been tempted to enhance the luster of the gospel, our pearl of great price, by placing it in a much too attractive setting. This may only detract from the true value of our pearl. Our pearl will stand on its own, with all of its beauty and simplicity. We do not need to enhance it with the bright and flashy things that will bring only antagonism and conflict to the Church. We need to speak less about our accomplishments, and by our actions we need to show which kingdom we seek.

Place on your refrigerator doors the scriptures that will continually remind you, as you go about your daily duties, who you are and what you represent. Could I suggest just a few of these scriptures as starters?

The first is Luke 6:35: "Love ye your enemies, and do good, and lend, hoping for nothing again; and your reward shall be great, and ye shall be the children of the Highest: for he is kind unto the unthankful and to the evil."

The second is James 1:27: "Pure religion and undefiled before God and the Father is this, To visit the fatherless and widows in their affliction, and to keep himself unspotted from the world."

Finally, display one of the great scriptures from the Book of Mormon, Moroni 7:47: "Charity is the pure love of Christ, and it endureth forever; and whoso is found possessed of it at the last day, it shall be well with him."

I love the gospel of our Lord and Savior. It has brought into my life the greatest peace of mind, joy, and happiness I could ever hope to imagine. I pray that we might all be willing and able to become peaceable followers of Christ.

NOTES

1. Thomas L. Kane, as quoted in *Memoirs of John R. Young, Utah Pioneer 1847* (Salt Lake City: Deseret News, 1920), pp. 31–33.

2. Robert Coles, *The Call of Service: A Witness to Idealism* (New York: Houghton Mifflin Co., 1993), pp. 3–4.

3. Ibid., pp. 4–5.

4. Ibid., p. 5.

5. Ibid., p. 51.

INDEX

Emerson, Ralph Waldo, 4
Enthusiasm, author cultivated talent of, 5–7
Evans, Richard L., on worth of individuals, 71
Eve, parental role of, 102
Example, importance in world, 61

Faith, strengthened by celebrations, 79
Family, importance of, 40–42, 101–2
Family life, replaced by TV, 101–2
Family home evening, 103–6
Fathers, duties of, 41–42
Fear, preparation frees one from, 23
Fifty, celebrations tied to number, 78
Finances, 99–100
Friendship, 49–55; benefits and dangers of, 49; ways to develop, 54
"Fulness of Times, The" (set of records), 35

General Authorities, lead exemplary lives of virtue, 44
Grant, Heber J., 123; dedicated meetinghouse, 11; on self-reliance, 96
Gratification, dangers of instant, 43

Habits, 74
Haggai, 39–40
Hebrew history, similarities to Church history, 77–82
Hickok, Eliza M., "Prayer" (poem), 30
Higgins, Professor Henry, 114
Home, the key to reverence, 13
Honesty, 73
Hubbard, Charles, 36, 37
Husbands, duties of, 41–42

Instant gratification, results of, 22
Institute, 51
Integrity, 72
Investments, 100

Jacob, Book of Mormon prophet: on possessions and pride, 33–34; on riches, 43
Jacob, father of Joseph, 1
James, on pure religion, 45
Jesus Christ: and Peter, 113–14; on profanity, 116; on proper language, 117
Job, 72
Johnson, Samuel, on habits, 74
Joseph, son of Jacob: early relationship with brothers, 1–2; experiences in Egypt, 2–4; interpreted Pharaoh's dream, 3–4
Jubilee year, 78, 81–82

Kane, Thomas L., on Nauvoo, 125–26
Kimball, Heber C., left family to go on mission, 35–37
Kimball, Spencer W.: on the oil of preparedness, 22–23; on sharing the gospel, 66; on decisions, 110; on profanity, 116
Kimball, Vilate, 36

Labor, joy of, 89–94
Last Supper, 113
Latter-day Saints, challenges facing, 64–65
Lee, Harold B.: on Lehi's vision, 25; on family home evening, 103
Lehi, comes to Bountiful, 95
Lehi's dream, 21–22, 43
Limhi, 120
Lincoln, Abraham, 73
Logan Temple, 83

Marines, 51
Marriage, ordained of God, 41
Materialism, effects of, 42–43
McKay, David O.: on parents' responsibilities to children, 17; on happiness in the home, 42; on friendship, 49; on solving world